Once in a while, a cookbook comes along that is so much more than a collection of recipes: It heralds a new voice that captures the now along with the breathtaking sweep of culture and tradition. We're given something familiar yet entirely new . . . and delicious.

Behold: the date. It is sweetness epitomized, a fruit of pure bliss and nutritious energy. An elemental, practical, humble bundle of caramelly goodness that lends itself to a world's worth of recipes and millennia of reverence.

HOT DATE! is big on flavor and low on fuss, full of recipes that combine the date's superfood status with playful, unpretentious, and highly cookable recipes. But it's not just a cookbook of 100 sweet and savory recipes featuring dates. It's a multisensory treasure trove that's also

+ **a kaleidoscopic feast for the mind and the eyes and the palate**

+ **a lavishly illustrated lookbook, humming with sensual, vibrant art and more than 35 beautiful photographs**

+ **a primer on dozens of date varieties available in the United States, the Middle East, North Africa, and across the globe**

+ **a travel diary alive to the sights, scents, and sounds of date groves around the world**

+ **an ode to the date that draws inspiration from historic oddities, luscious poetry, and more.**

Welcome to the oasis. We think you'll like it here.

HOT DATE!

Sweet & Savory
RECIPES
Celebrating
the **DATE,**
from
PARTY FOOD
to **EVERYDAY**
FEASTS

HOT DATE!

Text and Illustrations by
Rawaan Alkhatib

Photographs by
Linda Xiao

CHRONICLE BOOKS
SAN FRANCISCO

Library of Congress Cataloging-in-Publication Data available.

ISBN 978-1-7972-2644-6

Manufactured in China.

Prop styling by MAEVE SHERIDAN.
Food styling by MONICA PIERINI.
Design by VANESSA DINA.
Typesetting by WYNNE AU-YEUNG.

10 9 8 7 6 5 4 3 2 1

Chronicle books and gifts are available at special quantity discounts to
corporations, professional associations, literacy programs, and other
organizations. For details and discount information, please contact our
premiums department at corporatesales@chroniclebooks.com or at
1-800-759-0190.

Chronicle Books LLC
680 Second Street
San Francisco, California 94107
WWW.CHRONICLEBOOKS.COM

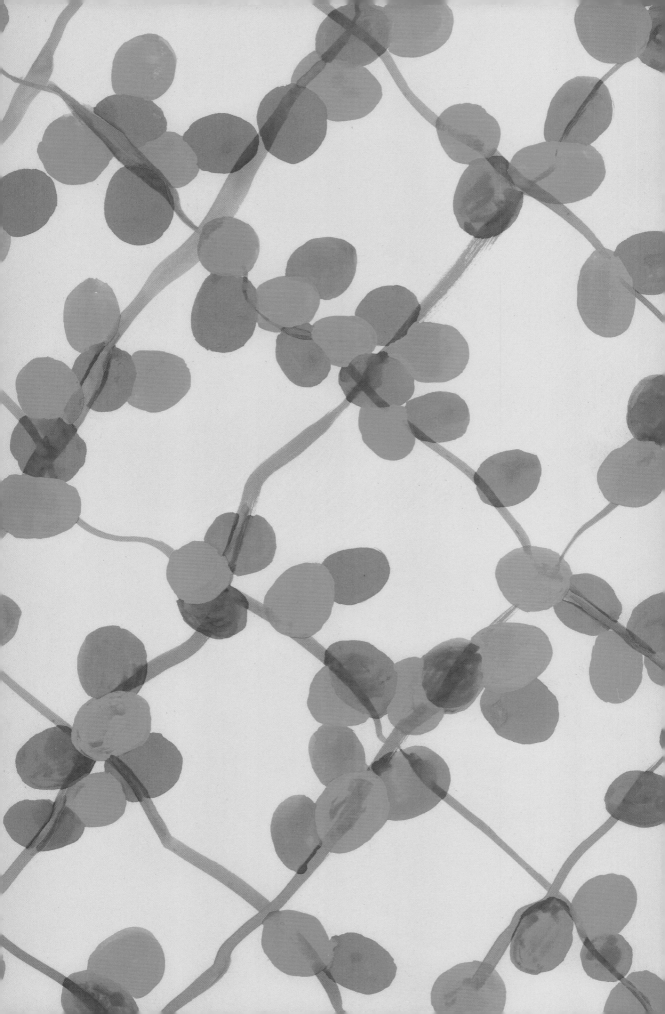

I had another introduction prepared, a more soulful one that hit all the right notes: the Noble Date! A most exquisite and ancient fruit! The sustenance of civilizations and the joy of many a hungry traveler! Naught can rival its cultural impact! And so on. We'll get to all that, I promise. But it started to get in the way of what I really want to tell you, which is that when you are standing in the shade of a date palm, your face obscured by feathery shadows, the fronds waving above you like a living parasol against the heat and dust, you begin to realize what it means to have access to such bounty.

Dates have prevailed because they are delicious and because they thrive in places where people can appreciate the miracle they are. The date has occupied a place in the imagination and on the table of humankind for millennia, simultaneously one of the most elemental, practical foods and one of the most revered. Nutritionally dense, compact, easy to transport, and easy to preserve, the date is also a holy fruit, a symbol of generosity and abundance. Every part of the date palm—the fronds, the blossoms, the bark, the tender heart, and, above all, the fruit—can be transformed into something useful.

I grew up in Dubai, a coastal city a couple of hours from the immense red-orange sand dunes of the Empty Quarter, where date palms are a ubiquitous feature of the landscape. The streets are replete with plumy palms, their roots in the water and their heads in the fiery sky. Every summer, as mind-boggling heat sets in, these trees are ringed with heavy necklaces of ripening fruit, yellow and red and lucent brown.

We ate dates as an everyday snack and piled them high at celebrations and special occasions. I remember the dates of my youth with much nostalgia, but in recent years, I have been even more electrified by their potential as symbolic—and delectable—vessels of shared abundance. We give the gift of dates not to display wealth or elitism but to spread joy and sustenance. They are democratically delicious, eaten by and accessible to every member of the society I come from.

The date palm is arguably the most ancient cultivated tree in existence. There is archaeological evidence of humans deliberately planting dates as long ago as seven thousand years, on Dalma Island in the United Arab Emirates and as-Sabiyah in Kuwait. Throughout our collective history, dates and date palms recur. Take your pick of any deeply human symbol, concept, or metaphor—at some point, it's had a date palm attached to it. Across thousands of years, dates have been associated with love, fertility, childbirth, the night, mourning, the dead, magic, life, joy, infinity, and chaos. They are stand-ins for the concept of time, long life, the "road to the moon." Dates have provided succor to pregnant women: Millennia apart, both Leto, mother to the twin deities Apollo and Artemis, and Mary, mother of Jesus, supposedly labored beneath palm trees and ate dates to ease the pangs of childbirth. Sumerian legend holds that the date palm was the very first fruit tree, pollinated by a wily raven; when Assyrian military commanders wished to annihilate their enemies, they razed their date orchards to the ground.

The oldest recipes ever discovered, inscribed on clay tablets nearly four thousand years ago in Babylon, use dates. Throughout the history of the written recipe, dates appear. (I have illustrated some of the most intriguing historic recipes I've found—look for the oddities sprinkled throughout the book—but while they make for fascinating reading material, I can't vouch for them as reliable modern-day cooking instructions.) Over and over, we encounter the date palm: an ever-fruitful food source in arid conditions. The date palm is the tree of life.

The value of the date isn't confined to ancient history. Today, it is impossible to overstate how iconic the date is in contemporary Middle Eastern and Muslim culture. A universal symbol of generosity and abundance, it is mentioned in the Qur'an more often than any other fruiting plant. Throughout the month of Ramadan, a holy moon-span of fasting and feasting, dates are consumed across the Islamic world, eaten at the moment of sunset.

I ate a dizzying variety of dates during my youth in the United Arab Emirates, from the bright sweet Lulu to the brown butter–caramel Sukkari and the rich and honeyed Khalas. I savored the tannic crunch and extraordinary sun-gold color of khalal-stage Barhi dates on the stalk and devoured fudgy, soft rutab Barhis as a straight-from-the-freezer snack to rival the most decadent gelato. Now, living in New York City, I buy luminous Deglet Nour and king-sized California Medjool dates at my neighborhood grocery store, owned and run by a Palestinian family with an eye for excellent produce.

With this cookbook, I hope to give you a taste of the many possibilities of the date, of its versatility and global significance. In the recipes, I've pulled flavors and techniques from across the many cultures that revere the date, but I have also strayed freely, with the only constraint being that I use some product of the date palm, in any of its many formats—dried, molasses, jam, or sugar—and iterations—fresh and crunchy, chewy, or soft and custardy. With an enviably supercharged nutritional profile, dates have long been relegated to North American penance-style lists of good-for-you foods, but their nuance and subtlety make any dish sing, and they deserve to be highlighted and celebrated. We have used dates to enliven the most pedestrian dishes for millennia, after all, and their appeal has never waned. Today, more than three thousand date varieties are grown across the world, with more emerging all the time.

Dates have become indispensable to the way I approach a meal, whether I'm having a quiet night in or cooking up a feast for twenty friends. Endlessly adaptable and always delicious, dates make everything better. Welcome to the oasis. I hope you like it here.

AN ILLUSTRATED GUIDE TO SOME KEY DATE VARIETIES

"Indeed when in a fresh state, [dates] are so remarkably luscious that there would be no end to eating them were it not for fear of the dangerous consequences that would be sure to ensue."

—PLINY THE ELDER

Dates have been cultivated for thousands of years, and countless thousands of date varieties have been grown and eaten during that time. Most date palms are clones, planted from saplings that sprout at the base of each trunk. If you want to grow a brand-new variety, you have to plant a date seed. The trees you grow won't provide fruit until they're four or five years old, but, much like us humans, can take a full twenty-one years to begin to put forth their finest efforts. Unlike us, they can live as long as a hundred and fifty years. With proper care, each tree can produce up to 330 pounds [150 kg] of fruit in a single growing season.

A single male palm can pollinate up to fifty female palms, but it's the female palms that determine the variety of fruit. In 2005, scientists sprouted a two-thousand-year-old Judaean date seed. It grew into a stout male palm, named Methuselah for the biblical figure who lived to the ripe old age of 969. Methuselah's pollen was used to fertilize the flowers of Hannah, a female tree grown from another ancient seed. The dates they made together tasted like bread and caramel.

Because it takes palms years to start producing dates, it can be a gamble to plant a date seed instead of a sapling: There's no guarantee that the dates will be any good, and you will have waited several years to taste the fruit of your labors. Despite the risk, new date varieties with their own unique characteristics emerge all the time. In Egypt, for instance, date sellers have a tradition of naming their dates to catch the attention of busy shoppers and boost sales—back in 2009, a new, bestselling premium date was dubbed the "Obama," in contrast to the lower-quality (and much cheaper) "Bush."

Here is a sampling of some slightly more established date varieties you might find around the world today. It is by no means even close to comprehensive.

ABBADA

CALIFORNIA, UNITED STATES.

Discovered in 1936, growing wild in a riverbed in California's Imperial Valley, and now grown across the Coachella Valley. Black, thick-textured date with notes of chocolate and cream. Very sweet.

AJWA

MEDINA, KINGDOM OF SAUDI ARABIA.

Revered across the Islamic world as the "holy date," considered the Prophet Mohammed's favorite variety. Glossy, dark, almost-black date, with a network of very fine wrinkles and a dry, soft texture. Mildly sweet, with flavors of prune, cinnamon, caramel, and dark honey.

ALIG

TUNISIA.

Moderately sweet, mahogany-colored, semidry, and wrinkly date. Soft in texture and distinctive in taste, with slightly more acidity than most date varieties.

AMIR HAJJ

MANDALI OASIS, IRAQ.

Very soft and extraordinarily sweet date. Thin-skinned, plump, and deep amber in color, with notes of caramel and warm spices, including cinnamon, cardamom, and nutmeg. Too soft to stuff or cook but makes an exceptional base for jams and syrups.

ANBARA

MEDINA, KINGDOM OF SAUDI ARABIA.

Firm and fleshy date, named for its reddish-brown color—"anbara" means "amber." Very large date that resembles a long, thick finger. Finely structured skin and notes of cinnamon sugar and burnt marshmallow; an excellent date for stuffing. Difficult to find, even in KSA, and considered an excellent gift.

ASEEL

KHAIRPUR MIRS, PAKISTAN.

Large, mild, dark brown date, with a chewy, semidry texture and a lightly caramelized flavor. The pride of Sindh province; 90 percent of the dates grown in Pakistan are of this variety.

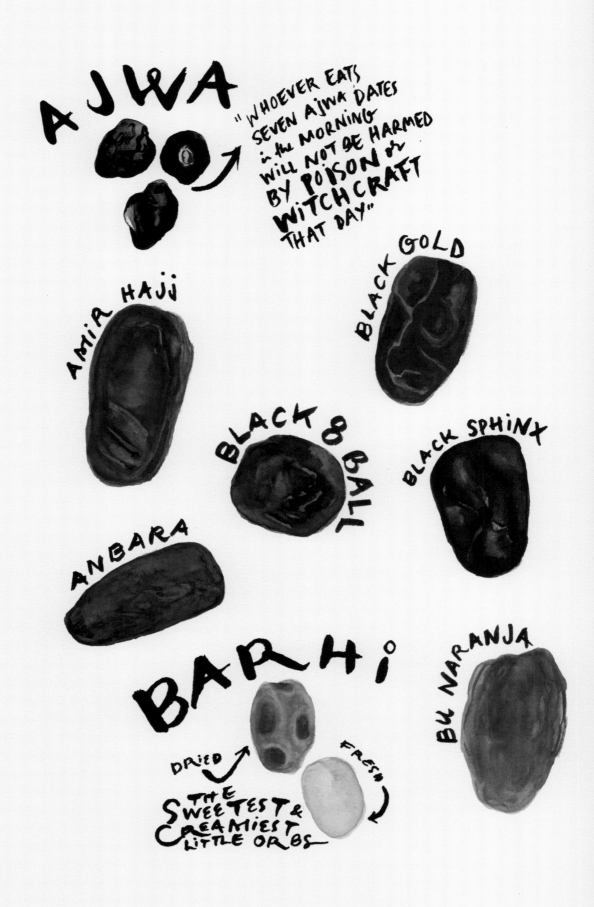

AJWA

"WHOEVER EATS SEVEN AJWA DATES in the MORNING WILL NOT BE HARMED BY POISON or WITCHCRAFT THAT DAY."

AMIR HAJJ

BLACK GOLD

BLACK 8 BALL

BLACK SPHINX

ANBARA

BARHI

DRIED → ← FRESH

THE SWEETEST & CREAMIEST LITTLE ORBS

BU NARANJA

BOUFEGGOUS

DEGLET NOUR

CONFITERA

DHAKKI

KHALAS

EMPRESS

BEST SERVED WITH ARABIC COFFEE

POP INTO THE FREEZER for a LUSCIOUS SUMMER TREAT!

CIRÉ

HALAWY

DAYRI

BARHI

BASRA, IRAQ.

Named for the regional "barh," or hot summer wind, and now grown worldwide. Among the varieties that can be eaten at the crunchy khalal stage, as well as when fully ripe, as they are far less astringent and tannic than most dates. At the khalal stage, Barhi are a beautiful, smooth yellow with a crisp, apple-like crunch and notes of coconut water, cinnamon, and sugarcane. Once fully ripe, Barhi darken to a luminous butterscotch-amber color; they are sweeter, with notes of buttered brown sugar and very ripe persimmon. The dates are smallish and round, with a creamy, smooth texture. This is a date that reminds you it's a fruit as you're eating it.

BARKAWI

SUDAN.

Unusually long and thin date that ranges in color from golden brown to reddish-brown. Sweet and juicy flesh. One of the most widely grown varieties in Sudan.

BARNI

KINGDOM OF SAUDI ARABIA.

Also widely grown in Oman. Medium-large date, with thin, glossy skin and a firm, long body. Golden brown, fibrous flesh, with a tangy aftertaste.

BEGUM JANGI

BALOCHISTAN PROVINCE, PAKISTAN.

Short little dates, soft and syrupy, with very thin skin. Exquisitely sweet. Named for Begum Jangi, wife of the Khan of Kalat, who is believed to have introduced the date palm to the region in the nineteenth century.

BERBEN

IRAQ.

Ruby red dates that are harvested and eaten at the crunchy khalal and custardy rutab stages, as they are too moisture-filled to ripen to the tamar stage without rotting.

BLACK 8 BALL

CALIFORNIA, UNITED STATES.

Dark, round date, nearly as black as its namesake. Sweet and semisoft, with a nutty flavor. A cultivar by Ben Laflin, a plant pathologist who grew a mix of date seeds in the early twentieth century at the Oasis Date Gardens ranch in the Coachella Valley.

BLACK GOLD

CALIFORNIA, UNITED STATES.

Soft, very dark, and slightly chewy date. Hints of chocolate, vanilla, dark cherry, and coffee coupled with an elusive je ne sais quoi. A cultivar by date farmer Sam Cobb from the Coachella Valley.

BLACK LAFLIN

CALIFORNIA, UNITED STATES.

Medium-sized, jet-black date with a creamy, moist texture and skin that melts into the flesh. Mildly sweet. One of the first varieties planted by Ben Laflin in Coachella Valley in the early twentieth centry.

BLACK MCGILL

CALIFORNIA, UNITED STATES.

Medium-sized, soft date with smooth black skin and flesh. Rich raisin-like flavor with notes of sweet butter and licorice. Grown from a seedling of unknown parentage by D.E. McGill in Mecca, California.

BLACK SPHINX

ARIZONA, UNITED STATES.

Plump, tender date with melting flesh and very dark mahogany skin. Notes of caramel, honey, and vanilla. Extremely rare and highly perishable; shipped and sold at the rutab stage. The only Arizona date variety, discovered as a rogue seedling growing in someone's yard in suburban Phoenix in 1928. On the Ark of Taste's list of culturally significant and endangered foods.

BLOND BEAUTY

CALIFORNIA, UNITED STATES.

Rare North American variety with soft and melting flesh, somewhat similar to Deglet Nour. Notes of taffy and sweet cream. From the Coachella Valley, on the Ark of Taste's list of culturally significant and endangered foods.

BOUFEGGOUS

MOROCCO.

Translates to "father of the cucumber," although no one knows why. Very aromatic, slightly elongated dates, with luminous light brown flesh and tasting notes of pale caramel. Particularly popular in southeastern Morocco.

BU NARANJA

OMAN.

Bu Naranja means "father of the orange," a reference to this variety's unique color. Otherwise similar in appearance to the Khalas date. Oblong and medium-large with thin, smooth flesh and a sweet and slightly tangy taste.

CIRÉ

CALIFORNIA, UNITED STATES.

Unusually chewy, almost granular date, with textured, pillowy skin. Not too sweet, with notes of citrus.

CONFITERA

ALICANTE, SPAIN.

Grown in the UNESCO World Heritage Site of el Palmeral de Elche, or Palmerar d'Elx, the northernmost date grove in the world and the only European commercial producer of dates. Brought to Spain hundreds of years ago during Islamic rule on the Iberian Peninsula. Often sold at the rutab stage, when they are plump, glossy, and distinguished by ombré coloring running from yellow-gold to dark brown. Later, at the tamar stage, the dates mature to a deep reddish-brown. Soft and sweet, with a confectionary-like quality

DABBAS

UNITED ARAB EMIRATES.

One of the tiniest dates in the world, with correspondingly diminutive seeds. Golden or dark brown, with moderately sweet, smooth dry flesh.

DAYRI

BASRA, IRAQ.

Like an even more date-y Medjool. Large, luxurious-feeling fruit with thick, soft flesh. Sometimes called the "monastery date," possibly for its resemblance to the deep black cloaks worn by monks. Mildly sweet with an earthy finish.

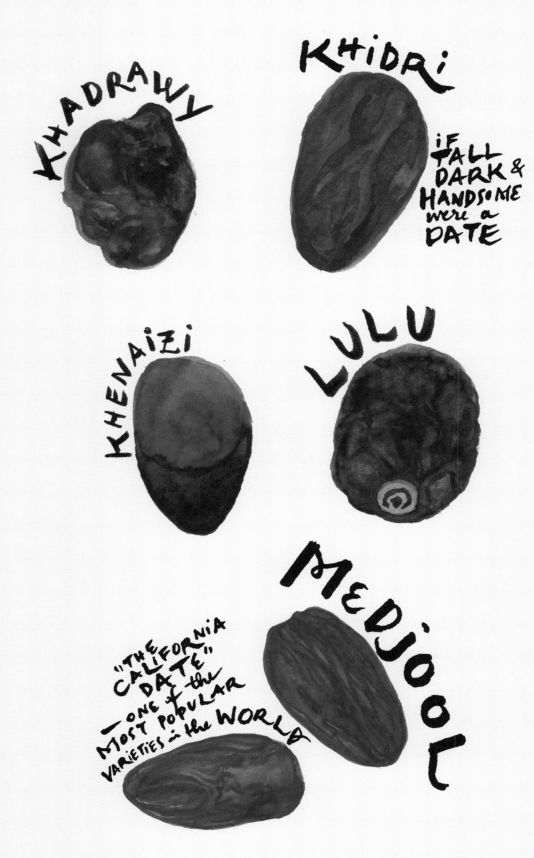

KHADRAWY

KHIDRI

iF TALL DARK & HANDSOME were a DATE

KHENAIZI

LULU

MEDJOOL

"THE CALIFORNIA DATE" —ONE of the MOST POPULAR VARIETIES in the WORLD

DEGLET NOUR

ALGERIA.

One of the most widely grown varietals in the world. Known as "fruit of the light" for their beautiful, luminous flesh, glowing with colors from butter to amber to gold. Semidry, with a slightly snappy crunch. Not very sweet, with notes of brown butter, toffee, and toasted cashew.

DHAKKI

PAKISTAN.

Grown in northwestern Pakistan and most often sold as fully dried dates, or chuara, with hard, wrinkled skin that keeps for even longer than dry tamar-stage dates. Richly rounded flavor and a distinctive yellowish color even when fully dried.

EMPRESS

CALIFORNIA, UNITED STATES.

Similar to Thoory dates but much softer. Moist, chewy, large, and distinctively shaped, with a pointed tip. A bi-colored variety named for its yellow-colored crown, which contrasts with its light gold or maroon flesh. From the Coachella Valley.

FARDH

OMAN.

Medium-large date with a comparatively tiny seed. Sweet and soft with smooth and glossy skin that is a very dark reddish-brown. The most commonly grown date in Oman.

HALAWY

BASRA, IRAQ.

Golden brown and wrinkly skinned, with sweet, chewy flesh that melts in the mouth, much like a piece of caramel—*Halawy* means "sweet" in Arabic. Notes of salty honey, raisins, and pecan pie.

KABKAB

IRAN.

Very sweet, velvety date, with unusually thick skin. Dark brown and semidry in texture.

KENTA

TUNISIA.

Commonly grown North African date, with golden brown skin and firm flesh. Moderately sweet with a very mild flavor.

KHADRAWY

IRAQ.

Small, stout date with paper-thin skin and mahogany-colored flesh that is simultaneously gooey and chewy. Highly prized for the silkiness of its melt-in-your-mouth texture; later in the season the date sugars crystallize for a pleasantly crunchy bite. Rich caramel flavor, with notes of fig, coconut, and molasses and a buttery aftertaste. An exceptional snacking date.

KHAISAB

UNITED ARAB EMIRATES.

Soft black date with a rounded, rich sweetness. Often eaten at the khalal stage while still crunchy and a beautiful red color.

KHALAS

UNITED ARAB EMIRATES.

The ne plus ultra of dates. *Khalas* means "quintessence" or "ideal," and this highly prized variety is often the recipient of lavish praise. Semitranslucent, papery skin with red-gold to dark brown flesh peeking through from underneath. Complex flavor with notes of honey butter, roasted sweet potato, ripe sugarcane, and toasted caramel released in successive waves, with a nutty taffy finish.

KHENAIZI

UNITED ARAB EMIRATES.

One of the most prized Emirati date varieties. Firm and fleshy, with a balanced sweetness and dark brown, wrinkled skin. Also edible at the khalal stage, when the lipstick-red fruit is crispy and mild.

KHIDRI

EGYPT.

Very dark brown and wrinkly, like a giant raisin in both appearance and taste, with caramel notes to finish. Dry, chewy flesh with no flaking. A highly regarded variety.

KHISTAWI

IRAQ.

Creamy-textured date with a syrupy flavor. Sweet and sticky with a soft, chewy, near-fiberless texture and thin, flaky, dark brown skin. An ancient variety that is popular in Baghdad, but otherwise hard to find due to its delicate skin.

KHOLA

KINGDOM OF SAUDI ARABIA.

Toffee-colored, baggy-skinned date that tastes like caramel. Often served with gahwa, or Arabic coffee.

LULU

UNITED ARAB EMIRATES AND IRAN.

Like Barhi dates, Lulu dates are often eaten fresh at the khalal stage, when they are a beautiful honey yellow, crisp, mild, and almost sugarcane-like in taste and texture. When fully dry, they are sweet and soft, like little toffees. Oval, wrinkled, dark brown. Very popular in the UAE.

MABROOM

KINGDOM OF SAUDI ARABIA.

Long, slender date with wrinkled skin and no flakiness. Firm, chewy flesh with mild sweetness and a well-rounded flavor that's similar to Ajwa dates.

MAKTOUM

BAGHDAD, IRAQ.

Unusually large, luxurious date with thick, slightly sticky reddish-brown skin. Delicious soft flesh, rich and subtle flavor, like a Medjool date.

MAZAFATI

IRAN.

Very deep black, juicy date with meaty flesh and a caramel-like taste. Notes of coffee and vanilla. Truly exquisite and considered the king of Iranian dates. Primarily grown in the ancient city of Bam, in the Kerman province of Iran.

MEDJOOL

MOROCCO.

A plump, meaty date, ranging in size from mini to super jumbo. Medjools are soft, with sweet flesh reminiscent of honey, cinnamon, and vanilla. One of the most popular varieties in the world, the Medjool originated from a single date palm in the Bou Denib oasis in the Tafilalet region of Saharan Morocco, where the variety is still known as "mejhool," or "unknown." The deliciousness of the Medjool has been a central attraction of the region for centuries, the date's praises sung by medieval Arab travelers who turned the variety into a principal export to Europe beginning in the seventeenth century. The variety was nearly wiped out due to a devastating date palm disease in the early twentieth century; the US Department of Agriculture imported eleven disease-free offshoots and grew them under quarantine in a remote region of Nevada for several years, where they were cared for by members of the Chemehuevi tribe. They are now grown heavily in California, particularly in the Coachella Valley, from which an estimated 90 percent of the dates grown in the United States come. The Medjool was also reintroduced to Morocco and is now grown across North Africa and beyond.

MIGRAF

YEMEN.

A huge amber-yellow date with a sweet and pleasant flavor. Migraf dates are particularly prized in southern Yemen for their exceptional quality.

PIAROM

IRAN.

Long and slender dates with nearly black, thin, wrinkly skin. Also known as "chocolate dates," Piaroms are opulent and sophisticated, with velvety, fudgy flesh that tastes like an unparalleled blend of coffee, caramel, and molasses. Particularly nutritious, they are highly prized across Iran and primarily grown in the province of Hormozgan.

RABBI

IRAN.

Long, reddish-black, oval-shaped dates, grown in Iran and Pakistan. Semidry, with meaty flesh and a lovely caramel flavor and aroma. Rabbi dates are particularly long-lasting due to their low moisture levels.

SEGAI

SOFT & JUICY

CRUNCHY

UNIQUE
Bi-COLORED
VARIETY

SUKKARI

"SUGARY"
"IN"
ARABIC

DENSE,
SUGARY,
CRYSTALLINE
FLESH—A
ROYAL DATE

SAFAWI

MEDINA, KINGDOM OF SAUDI ARABIA.

Medium-sized, deep black cherry–colored, and glossy, with intensely sweet flesh slightly reminiscent of coffee. Semidry, moist, and chewy-soft. Safawi trees are particularly high-yielding, so the dates are commercially available year-round in KSA.

SAMANI

EGYPT.

When dry, Samani dates have dark brown flesh with a plush cushion of light amber brown skin and a butterscotch flavor. The variety is low enough in tannins to be eaten fresh at the khalal stage, when still crispy and light orange or yellow, with a long, smooth oval shape.

SAYER

IRAN AND UNITED ARAB EMIRATES.

Reddish-brown, semidry dates with a soft texture and flaky skin. Particularly sweet, with the ripe, dark brown variety clocking in at a 75 percent sugar content.

SEGAI

RIYADH, KINGDOM OF SAUDI ARABIA.

A two-for-one bi-textured and bi-colored variety: pale gold, dry, and crunchy at the tip but otherwise meltingly soft and toffee brown. Medium-sized, Segai dates are an unconventional and particularly appealing date.

SIWI

SIWA OASIS, EGYPT.

The original Egyptian date variety, from the ancient oasis of Amun-Ra in the northwestern Egyptian desert, located between the Qattara Depression and the Great Sand Sea. This golden brown date has fragile skin and very succulent, sweet flesh.

SUKKARI

KINGDOM OF SAUDI ARABIA.

Sukkari means "sugary" in Arabic; when fully dry this variety is characterized by the delicious sugary crystals that form in its flesh and a melt-in-the mouth, chewy texture. Lovely flavor of mild caramel, fresh sugarcane, and young coconut water. Pale gold in color, these almost-crisp dates originate from Al Qassim region of KSA; they are prized across the Arabian Peninsula and often referred to as the "royal date."

TAFEZOUINE

ALGERIA.

A tasty, soft, and fleshy date, cylindrical in shape and shiny in appearance. Commercially grown in the regions of Touggourt, Ouargla, and Ghardaia.

TARBAZAL

CALIFORNIA, UNITED STATES.

A rare date with a fun backstory: The last known trees in the United States were found abandoned in the parking lot of an old auto body shop in Mecca, California, and rescued by a local date farmer. Offshoots have gradually spread across the Coachella Valley and are starting to become commercially available, though they are still hard to find. Large, oblong fruit with a deep unfurling of layers of caramel.

THOORY

ALGERIA.

Also known as the "bread date," this dry date is chewy and less sticky than other varieties, with a mild, almost peanutty sweetness and a texture reminiscent of pastry. Firm and golden brown with very wrinkly skin. Often touted as "the date you can put in your pocket," since its textural integrity means it won't ooze out and cause outfit chaos. Need a pocket date for whenever a snack impulse strikes? Try a Thoory; you won't regret it.

WANAN

KINGDOM OF SAUDI ARABIA.

Soft, wrinkly dates, long and conical in shape. Mildly sweet, with a spicy, almost cinnamon-like taste and aroma.

ZAGHLOUL

EGYPT, THE GAZA STRIP, AND THE KUTCH DISTRICT OF INDIA.

Gorgeous long red dates, commonly eaten fresh at the crunchy khalal stage (like yellow Barhi dates). At harvest time, they look like spectacular bunches of enormous, shiny red grapes dangling from long yellow stems. Glossy, smooth, deep red or burgundy skin and crisp, bright white fiberless flesh. Khalal-stage Zaghlouls are mildly astringent, with flavors of sweet spices, warm cinnamon, and sugarcane. Particularly prized in Egypt, where they share the name of a national hero, revolutionary statesman Saad Zaghloul.

ZAHIDI

IRAQ.

Pale brown, medium-sized dates with thick skin
and dry, chewy golden flesh. Notes of dried apricot, caramel corn, and toasted nuts. Occasionally known as the "butter date" due to its mild
flavor and pale color. *Zahidi* means "ascetic" in
Arabic, a comment perhaps on its relatively mild
sweetness.

ZAMLI

NAMIBIA.

Originally from Saudi Arabia. Zamli dates are
eaten at all three stages of ripeness. Small and
soft, with deeply wrinkled skin. Zamlis have a
melted caramel flavor and toffee-textured flesh;
their sweetness is so pronounced that they are
often referred to as "nature's caramel."

THOORY

SIWI

KANAN

ZAGHLOUL

ZAHIDI

ZAMLI

THE MANY FORMS OF THE DATE

Dates come in many formats. Here are a few of the most common.

DATES

Dates are considered edible in three stages—the crunchy khalal stage, the custardy rutab stage, and the chewy tamar stage—but are mostly found at the grocery store in the tamar stage, in which they are dry but not dried. A fully ripe date on the vine has an extremely low moisture content, so even though it is technically a fresh fruit, it is still very shelf-stable. Chopped dates (dates that have been pre-chopped and dusted in flour to prevent sticking) can often be found languishing in the baking aisle. Frankly, these weird nubbins give dates a bad name. Avoid if you can!

DATE CRYSTALS

Dehydrated date slivers, about the size of oatmeal flakes, that must be reconstituted in liquid to be used as an equivalent for chopped dates.

DATE JAM

Spreadable version of date paste; loose, glossy, and more like a fruit butter than a fruit jam.

DATE JUICE

Sweet sap that was traditionally collected by shaving the bark of the date palm to encourage the flow of the sap into earthen jars hung to collect the juice overnight. Now more commonly made by soaking dates in water (or sometimes milk), then blending them. Both formats are ideal for combatting summertime dehydration.

DATE MOLASSES

Also known as date honey, date nectar, date syrup, dhibs or dibs, rubb or robb, or silan. One of the oldest sweeteners used by humans. The Babylonians called it "honey" and used it to sweeten foods to offer to gods and royalty. It's made by either boiling, puréeing, and straining dates or using an old-school cold-press method, in which the dates are compressed and their juices allowed to run out. Many old houses in the Arabian Peninsula are equipped with a madbasa, or molasses room, with clay-coated walls and floors that slope down to a sunken tank in the floor. Using a technique dating back to at least the second millennium BCE, people pile ripe dates around the room and allow the juices to ooze out under their own weight and flow down into the central tank. If buying, make sure that the only ingredients are dates and water; there shouldn't be any additional sweeteners.

DATE PASTE

Pitted, compressed dates, packed into cakes. Extremely shelf-stable and can be purchased as dense bricks and kept for up to two years if unopened and stored in a cool, dry place.

DATE SUGAR

Made from whole dates, dehydrated and ground up, date sugar is similar in appearance to brown sugar but much less sweet, with a toasty, subtly caramelized flavor. Substitute measure for measure in baked goods but know that it will not fully dissolve in liquids.

DATE VINEGAR

Sweet-and-sour vinegar that's mild and aromatic. Use it anywhere you would use an apple cider vinegar or similarly fruity vinegar.

DRIED DATES

Also called kharak or chuara. Dates in this form are fully dehydrated, leathery, wrinkled, and chewy; they last indefinitely and need to be soaked in liquid before being consumed.

ANATOMY of a DATE PALM

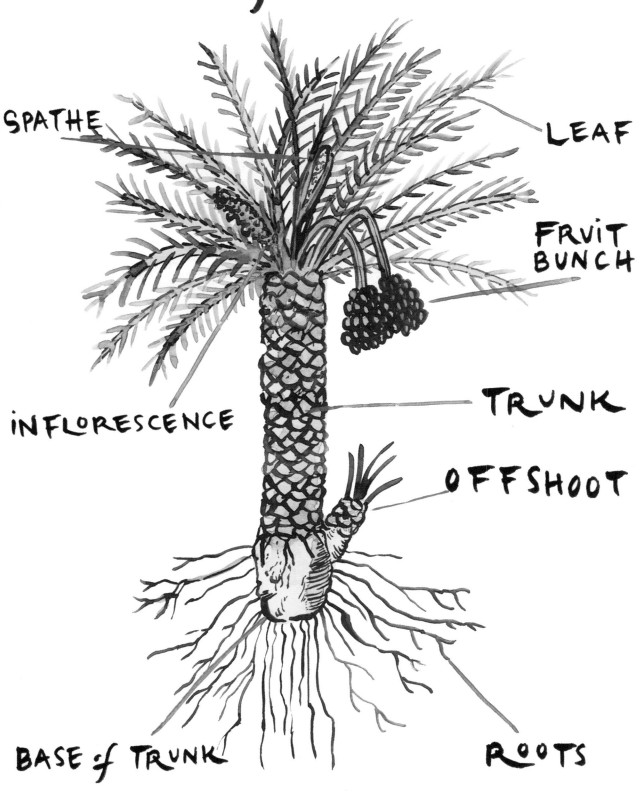

SPATHE

LEAF

FRUIT BUNCH

INFLORESCENCE

TRUNK

OFFSHOOT

BASE of TRUNK

ROOTS

STORING DATES

Fresh dates at the both the khalal and rutab stages are very delicate. Treat them as you would a fresh fruit. They last a maximum of six to twelve days without refrigeration, but they are best stored cold in an airtight container in the refrigerator or freezer, which will prolong their shelf life by weeks and to up to six months in the freezer.

Semidry dates at the tamar stage are medium-soft. Most dates at the grocery store fall into this category. They keep at room temperature for several weeks, but for best results, store them in the refrigerator for up to five months and in the freezer for up to twelve months.

Dry dates are hard and chewy. They will keep at room temperature for up to a year if stored in a cool, dry place, or even longer in the refrigerator or freezer.

MALE & FEMALE DATE BLOSSOMS

LONG, SLENDER FRAGRANT BLOSSOMS USED TO POLLINATE the FEMALE FLOWERS

FEMALE FLOWERS

THE VARIETY of DATE IS DETERMINED BY THE FEMALE TREE

MALE FLOWERS

SMALL ROUND FLOWERS THAT EVENTUALLY PRODUCE DATES

ONE MALE DATE PALM CAN POLLINATE UP TO 50 FEMALE TREES

The LIFE CYCLE of the DATE

LATE WINTER → EARLY Spring

MALE FLOWERS BLOOM. THEIR POLLEN is HARVESTED TO HAND-POLLINATE the FEMALE FLOWERS.

LATE SPRING → EARLY Summer

DATE BRANCHES ARE THINNED TO LEAVE ROOM for FRUIT TO GROW. BUNCHES ARE TIED for EVEN WEIGHT DISTRIBUTION; FRUIT IS BAGGED to PROTECT it.

LATE Summer → EARLY FALL

KHALAL-STAGE DATES ARE HARVESTED WHILE STILL CRUNCHY. THE REMAINING DATES ARE MONITORED AS THEY RIPEN; HARVEST PREPARATIONS ARE UNDERWAY.

FALL HARVEST TIME!

EACH BUNCH is VISITED MULTIPLE TIMES, AS DATES RIPEN AT DIFFERENT STAGES on the SAME BUNCH. RIPE DATES ARE WASHED, CLEANED & PACKAGED.

STAGES
OF DATE
RIPENESS

There's an Arabic saying about how to get your palm trees to grow the sweetest dates: Keep their feet in the water and their heads in the fires of hell. They thrive in the hottest, driest weather with plenty of water at their roots.

It takes about seven months for dates to fully ripen from flower to fruit, and that process has five distinct stages: hababuk, kimri, khalal, rutab, and tamar.

STAGE 1: HABABUK

The hababuk stage is when dates are pollinated, a labor-intensive process that is still conducted entirely by hand no matter how large the plantation. Male flower clusters can be cut from the tree and inserted into female clusters or their pollen can be shaken out and dusted with little puffers onto female clusters. In either case, once pollinated, female clusters are bagged up or otherwise protected.

STAGE 2: KIMRI

Dates are still very hard in the kimri stage, and a bright apple green. They start out the size of a small round berry, and mature until they are almost full-sized, though they remain green, hard, and bitter. Kimri is the longest stage of development and at this point, many date growers thin out the amount of fruit—sometimes up to 70 percent!—to give the dates room to grow. They also often tie the date bunches to the tree or otherwise bolster them to support the weight of the increasingly heavy ripening fruit.

"The offshoot should be planted by a man who possesses feminine qualities and a moist temperament. While planting it, he should laugh and be merry and tell jokes. If he is not in the mood, then he should at least pretend to be so. This will be good for the welfare of the growing date palm."

–FROM "NABATEAN AGRICULTURE" BY IBN WAHSHIYYA
(TENTH CENTURY CE, BAGHDAD)

STAGE 3: KHALAL

By the khalal stage, the fruit is fully mature and begins to undergo a color change, turning yellow, orange, pink, red, or scarlet, depending on the variety. The sugars in the date increase rapidly, but most types of dates are still too tannic to eat at this point. A few varieties can be harvested and eaten at this stage, such as Barhi or Zaghloul; they are mildly but pleasantly tannic and crunchy, with the crispness of an apple and a lingering subtle sweetness, like fresh sugarcane.

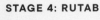

KHALAL الخلال

STAGE 5: TAMAR

Tamar-stage dates are what you find in the supermarket: still very sweet and juicy but fully dry. Although still harvested from the tree at this stage, the low moisture content of the fruit makes them naturally wrinkly and dried-looking. This is why we say that dates are a dry fruit, not a dried fruit. Dates have the highest sugar content at this point and are at their most shelf-stable, though they will still keep best in the refrigerator or freezer.

TAMAR التمر

STAGE 4: RUTAB

Fully ripe but still extremely moist, rutab-stage dates are delicate, translucent, and very juicy. As the fruit ripens and softens in ombré fashion, turning from yellow or red to brown, its tannins break down and the dates take on a luxurious melt-in-your-mouth texture, becoming very sweet. People often enjoy dates at this half-firm, half-soft stage for an exquisite contrast of sweetness and crunch.

RUTAB الرطب

THE HOT DATE! PANTRY

Here are ingredients I particularly love to cook with—
some may be more familiar to you than others. I hope you
find some new tastes as you work your way through this
book and that some of them become go-tos for you, too.

ALPHONSO MANGOES (HAPUS MANGO)

The King of Mangoes! Small fruit with skin
that shades from parrot green through to
saffron yellow—it's perfectly ripe when both
the skin and flesh are the color of a marigold
in full bloom. Remarkably sweet and juicy,
with near-fiberless flesh. A true alphonso
carries notes of jasmine and pine when fresh.
Originally from Goa, and widely grown across
India, but difficult to find in the United States
unless you have a hookup. I've heard tales
of clandestine WhatsApp groups that herald
the arrival of mango season with airfreight
dispatches, but you have to know a guy (or an
auntie) to get in on the game.

BLACK SESAME PASTE (BLACK TAHINI, BLACK SESAME BUTTER, KURO NERI GOMA, HEI ZHI MA JIANG)

Much like tahini but made with unhulled
black sesame seeds for an even richer and
nuttier flavor. Bitter enough to taste almost
burnt but in a very compelling and addictive
way. Use anywhere you would tahini, but
start sparingly at first. Chinese versions use
roasted sesame seeds for an even deeper
flavor.

BULGUR

Cracked parboiled wheat, an essential ingredient when making tabbouleh and useful to
the home cook for a whole galaxy of applica-
tions: You can use this nutty, fragrant whole
grain anywhere you would rice, couscous, or
quinoa. Particularly delightful on a weeknight, as its parboiled nature means it cooks
up very quickly. Commonly sold in one of
three grades: coarse, medium, or fine. The
finer the grade, the quicker it cooks.

CARDAMOM (ELAICHI, HAIL)

Papery spindle-shaped seed pods with
intensely flavored black seeds inside. A little
goes a long way. Best purchased and stored
as whole pods, because this spice quickly
loses its flavor once ground. Elusive notes
of resin, pine, licorice, and an almost minty
freshness. Mostly grown for export in India,
and in the cloud forests of Guatemala. Crack
a pod between your teeth and toss it into your
morning cup of tea or coffee.

CURRY LEAVES (KADI PATTA, KARIBEVU, MITHO LIMDO, KARUVEPILLAI, DAUN KARI, GĀLÍ YÈ, KA LEI YIP)

Not curry powder. A different beast (or plant) altogether. Nothing compares to curry leaves, and there's no substitute. Sorry, I don't make the rules! Dark, glossy green leaves with an extraordinary scent and a complex citrus-like flavor that is best coaxed out by toasting in some kind of fat. You can use dried whole or powdered curry leaves, but they are far more flavorful when fresh. They'll keep in your freezer, well wrapped, for long periods of time. I have been known to mail order a curry leaf plant in times of desperation, coddling a seedling on the windowsill of my Brooklyn apartment for as long as I can, but they do grow into actual trees when planted outdoors in the right conditions.

DESERT TRUFFLES (KAMAH, KEMA, KIMA, CHIMA, FAGGA, FAQ', TERFEZ, ZUBAIDI)

Imagine a sandy potato with an air of mystique: That's what a desert truffle is like, if you are lucky enough to find one. A delicacy found in springtime across the Mediterranean, Middle East, and North Africa and only distantly related to the European variety, desert truffles have the flavor of a deeply earthy mushroom with the texture of an artichoke heart. Highly seasonal, with folklore stating that they are spawned by thunderclaps and lightning strikes during the rainy season, these truffles are wild foods, foraged by experienced truffle hunters. Roast them in the ashes of your campfire if you happen across some on a desert camping trip.

FREEKEH

An ancient variety of Palestinian wheat that is harvested while it is still milky and green, then roasted over open fires to slough off the husks, and left to dry in the sun. This results in a grain with a remarkably tasty grass-smoke flavor and slightly chewy texture. Available in cracked or whole form: Cracked cooks faster; whole is denser and chewier. Traditionally used in soups, as a side dish, or as the foundational grain for an entire feast.

GHEE (SAMN, SAMNA, SAMNEH)

Make butter better by making it more buttery than butter. That's the secret to ghee, the Indian version of clarified butter, which is cooked down until all the water is gone and it tastes ever so slightly nutty and caramelized, then strained. Ghee is shelf-stable, with a high smoke point; you can use it to cook at a much higher temperature than you would with butter. Make it at home, or buy it by the jar from Indian grocery stores. A similar version, called samna, is the Arabic-speaking world's equivalent.

CURRY LEAF

MANGIFERA INDICA

ALPHONSO MANGO

MURRAYA KOENIGII

OLIVE

NIGELLA

NIGELLA SATIVA

ROSA DAMASCENA

DAMASK ROSE

RHUS CORIARIA

VANILLA PLANIFOLIA

VANILLA

MAKRUT

CITRUS HYSTRIX

HALWA (HALVA, HALVAH)

Halwa means "sweet" in Arabic. It's used throughout the book to refer to the sesame-based, fudge-like candy (dense, rich, and crumbly) as opposed to the jiggly cooked puddings of the Asian subcontinent and parts of the Arabian Peninsula.

HALWA FLOSS (PESHMEK, SHA'AR BANAT, GHAZL EL BANAT, PIŞMANIYE)

Variations on a spun sugar theme. Like cotton candy but whipped up out of fine threads of wheat or tahini halwa, or just sugar. Arabic, Iranian, and Turkish versions are all slightly different and uniformly delicious. Often sold sprinkled with finely ground pistachios.

LABNEH (LABNE, LABNA, LABANAH)

What yogurt wants to be when it grows up. Thick, salty, and voluptuous, labneh lands somewhere between a strained yogurt and a fresh cheese. You can make it at home or buy it in stores in spreadable form, or as little balls or cubes preserved in olive oil, often flavored with herbs and spices.

LOOMI (DRIED LIME, PERSIAN LIME, BLACK LIME, OMANI LIME, NOOMI BASRA, LIMOO AMANI)

Matte-black orbs with mysterious flavor-enhancing powers. Sun-dried whole limes from Oman, sour and earthy and slightly smoky. Can be grated or ground to a powder, or pierced and used whole. Often used to flavor fish, and to make a refreshing rosewater-enhanced dried limeade in the summertime. If you can't find loomi (though it is worth the trouble of a little quest), use the zest and juice of one fresh lime instead.

MAKRUT LIME LEAVES (THAI LIME LEAVES)

Dark-green, hourglass-shaped leaves, remarkably fragrant and intensely flavorful. An essential component of food across Southeast Asia. Used whole in cooking or de-ribbed and finely sliced. Available fresh, frozen, or dried; dried are markedly less fragrant, so you will need to increase the amount you use.

MASTIC

A resin. A joy. The hardened sappy tears of a Mediterranean shrub. The world's first chewing gum, and the etymological origin of the word "masticate." Piney. The best kind comes from the Greek island of Chios. If you can get your hands on some, crush a pebble or two into a fine powder and add to your morning coffee. Wow!

NIGELLA SEED (HABBA SAWDA, BLACK SEED, KALONJI)

If you ask my mother, she will tell you that this tiny teardrop-shaped seed can cure pretty much anything that's wrong with you—and she isn't alone in holding that belief. She once shipped me a bottle of black seed oil emblazoned with the phrase "CURES ANYTHING BUT DEATH." I'm not making any promises. All I can tell you is that they are extremely delicious, with a flavor that is a little bit onion and oregano, a little bit cumin— sharp and smoky and promising.

NUT AND SEED OILS

I like to keep a variety in stock in small, opaque vessels since nut oils are light-sensitive and will turn rancid if you don't use them up quickly enough. A good nut oil can transform a boring meal. Drizzle bright green pistachio oil over roasted beets and grapefruit chunks. Dress a lentil salad with walnut oil and coarsely ground mustard. Gloss a scoop of ice cream with pumpkin seed oil and a bit of flaky salt. The only thing better than pecan pie is pecan pie with whipped cream and a floater of roasted pecan oil. Sky's the limit.

NUTRITIONAL YEAST

An unfortunate name for a delicious substance; let us not even attempt to discuss the use of the word "nooch." These golden flakes (made of deactivated, dehydrated yeast) are umami powerhouses, with a cheesiness and savoriness that makes all kinds of foods sing. Use as a finishing sprinkle and flavor enhancer, much like Parmesan cheese or MSG.

OLIVE OIL

Buy it by the gallon. Use copiously, before it turns rancid: Olive oil should be poured with a heavy hand. My Palestinian grandmother swore by it as a panacea and would knock back a big spoonful every day. You'll want at least two bottles: the good stuff, for cooking and heavy-duty work, and the best stuff, extra-virgin cold-press, for drizzling and guzzling.

ORANGE BLOSSOM WATER

Distilled from bitter orange flowers; exquisite haunting scent and taste. Use it in sweet or savory dishes, or try an after-dinner digestif of Lebanese "white coffee": Tip a capful of orange blossom water into a cup of hot water, and savor every sip.

POMEGRANATE MOLASSES

A tangy, luscious syrup combining the unbridled power of sweet and sour, made from pomegranate juice boiled down to a tawny slick. Though it leans a little more savory than sweet, its uses are endless. Try it as a marinade, a salad dressing, and a glaze (for cake or for roast chicken—it's equally compelling in both capacities).

PRESERVED LEMON

Think of everything a lemon can do and then supercharge it. Preserved lemons, traditionally used in North African cooking, add more of everything: sourness, tang, brightness, and complexity, with a big salty oomph to round things out. They are not intended to be eaten on their own, but used as a seasoning to enliven everything they touch.

ROSEWATER

Summer in a bottle. Imagine wandering the paths of a rose garden, soft clustered petals vibrating with color, the lush, rich scent intensifying every time you bring your face to a flower to quaff down the smell, the heat haze drifting around you . . . then bottle that smell, that taste, that feeling. Distilled from damask roses, delicate rosewater is used in both sweet and savory dishes; you only need a little bit to make a meal feel very special. Use the best you can find, since substandard rosewater will just make your dishes taste like soap.

SAFFRON

The most expensive spice in the world, harvested from delicate purple crocuses that only bloom for one week a year. The flowers must be handpicked at midmorning before they unfurl in order to protect their fragile cargo: three luminous red stigmas, which must then be plucked out by hand and gently processed. It takes about seventy-five thousand flowers to produce a pound of saffron—imagine a football field covered in pale purple blossoms—which is why it's usually sold by the gram. There really isn't anything like it, though—its intoxicating aroma is heady, honeyed, charged, and the lucent yellow-orange hue it lends food is almost as beautiful as its slightly bitter, elusively earthy taste. Most of the saffron produced today is grown in Iran, though it is also commercially grown in Spain, Turkey, Greece, Afghanistan, and Kashmir.

SUMAC

The dried berries of the sumac plant, cured and coarsely ground into a tangy, red-purple souring agent. It's one of the cornerstone ingredients of musakhan, the national dish of Palestine, and is used across the Middle East, Mediterranean, and Iran. Sprinkle it anywhere you would use a squeeze of lemon juice, to brighten and amplify: on rice, over fresh fruit, in a marinade for meat, on a salad (like fattoush), over eggs or grilled vegetables . . .

TAHINI

Made from sesame seeds, toasted and hulled and ground into a paste. A vital part of a truly iconic breakfast: mix tahini and date molasses in a shallow saucer and serve as a dip for warm pita bread.

URFA BIBER

A sun-dried Turkish chile that is coarsely ground into irregular purplish flakes and cut with oil and salt, so it functions more like a condiment than a pure chili powder. Smoky, almost chocolaty, with a fruity saltiness that's like nothing else.

VANILLA BEANS

I know it seems counterintuitive to include something as seemingly commonplace as vanilla on a list of (arguably) more esoteric ingredients. But did you know that the beans grow on a vining orchid? It's one of the only orchids to produce a foodstuff that's edible to humans. Native to Mexico and first harvested by the Aztecs, vanilla is now grown across the world. It's one of the most labor-intensive and sought-after spices in cultivation. Each flower blooms for a single day and needs to be hand-pollinated to produce a vanilla bean. Researchers have recently found that both breast milk and baby formula have strong vanilla fragrance compounds—so we associate the smell with nurture, food, and warmth from our very earliest days, explaining perhaps why it is such a universally popular ingredient.

YUZU KOSHO

A fermented Japanese hot sauce, this thick paste is made from salt, chile, and the zest and juice of the yuzu citrus. It's complex, fruity, briny, and delightfully spicy—a little goes a long way. A tiny jar in your fridge will last indefinitely.

ADDITIONAL
INGREDIENT NOTES

Unless otherwise noted:

- Butter is unsalted.
- Salt is Diamond Crystal Kosher Salt.
- Sugar is white granulated sugar.
- Eggs are large.
- Olive oil is extra-virgin.
- Flour is all-purpose.

... ONE NIGHT I CREPT PAST HER BROTHERS' TENTS
       THEY WOULD LIKE TO BOAST of KILLING ME
          AND ARRIVED AT HER CHAMBER

THE PLEIADES FLASHED in the SKY
       LIKE GEMSTONES in a WHIRLING KILT

I WENT IN
       SHE HAD TAKEN OFF ALL HER CLOTHES
          EXCEPT HER NIGHTGOWN

SO I TOOK HER OUT FOR A WALK
       AND SHE DRAGGED A HEAVY SKIRT BEHIND US
          ERASING OUR PRINTS

WE LEFT HER PEOPLE'S CAMP
       AND HEADED for the OPEN DESERT
          DIM HOLLOWS and TWISTING SANDS

I PULLED HER DOWN BY HER SIDELOCKS
       SHE BENT OVER ME
          SLIM HIPS and BIG ANKLES

SHE IS LEAN and BLAZINGLY WHITE
       TAUT-BELLIED
          HER BREASTS SHINE LIKE A MIRROR

SHE TURNS and SHOWS A SMOOTH CHEEK
A WARY EYE
THIS MOTHER GAZELLE at WAJRA

A SHOCK of HAIR BLACK as BURNT WOOD
THICK and CLUSTERED
LIKE A DATE PALM HEAVY WITH FRUIT

SHE PUTS IT UP BUT IT IS STILL A WILDERNESS
SOME in BRAIDS   SOME COMBED STRAIGHT

A THIN WAIST LIKE the NOSE HALTER I PUT ON MY CAMEL
PLUMP THIGHS LIKE STALKS of WATERED PAPYRUS

SHE STRETCHES OUT HER FINGERS
TRIMMED of MEAT LIKE SANDWORMS
OR TAMARISK TOOTHPICKS

AT DUSK SHE LIGHTS UP the DARKNESS
RADIANT AS A LONE MONK'S LANTERN ...

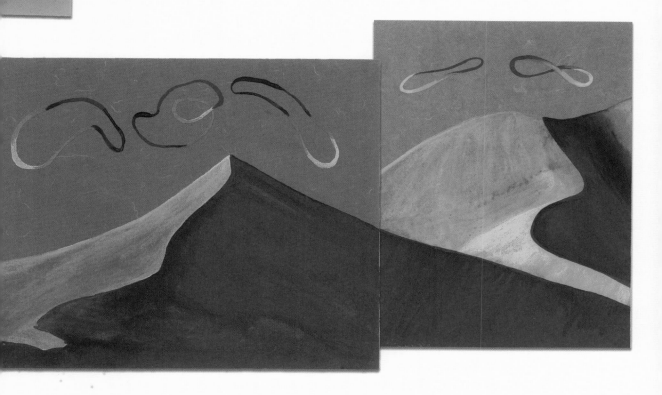

from "THE SUSPENDED ODE"
or "MU'ALLAQA" of IMRU AL-QAYS
translated by ROBYN CRESWELL

PARTY
FOOD

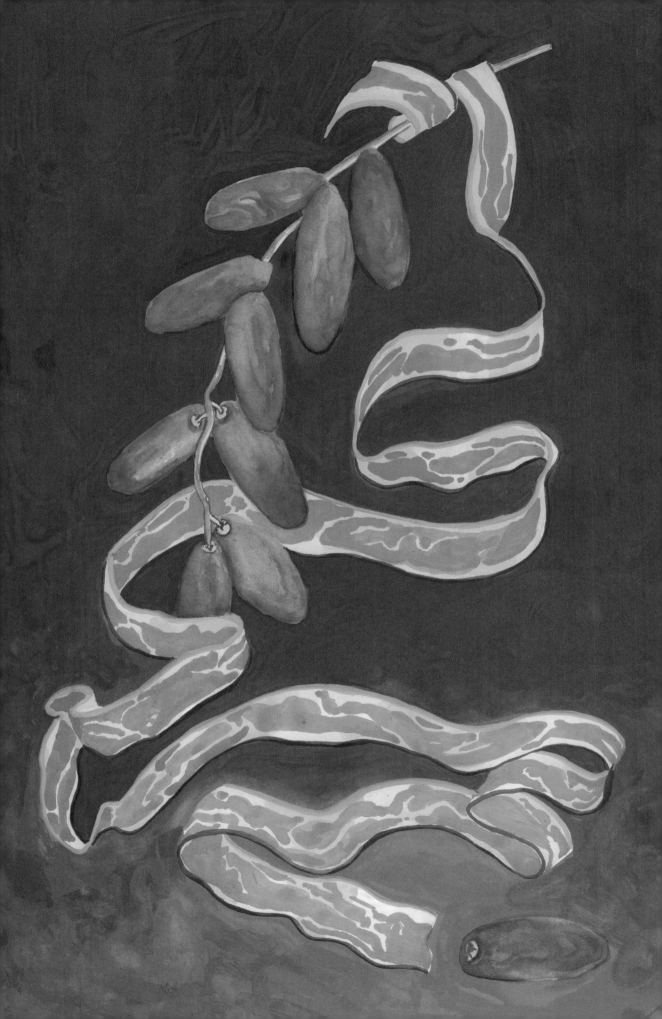

BACON-WRAPPED DATES

20 DATES (MULTIPLIES EASILY)

Might as well start with the crème de la crème of date recipes, right? Here is a three-ingredient winner for you to bust out at a gathering of any size. Though the recipe makes twenty dates, you can multiply as needed; just know that one slice of bacon can be used to swaddle two dates.

Although this is an easy assembly-line situation, there are a couple of things you can do to make the dates extra-special. Start cooking the dates in a cold oven to give the bacon fat time to render without overcooking the dates. Look for the thinnest bacon you can find. I ask my local butcher to use the prosciutto setting on their slicer to get the bacon as thin as possible. You can absolutely use regular cut store-bought bacon, but the ethereal quality of the wafer-thin slices is very pleasing. The cheese is optional but encouraged. Try experimenting with other stuffings, or just wrap plain dates in bacon; no one will complain. Finally: If you can find lamb bacon, use it!

20 dates of your choice, pitted

4 oz [115 g] hard aged cheese, such as Pecorino Romano, Manchego, or Parmesan, cut into ½ in [13 mm] wide, date-length batons

10 thinly cut bacon slices

Flaky salt

Freshly ground black pepper

Line a rimmed baking sheet with parchment paper.

Stuff each date with a baton of cheese and gently squeeze the dates closed around the cheese.

Cut each slice of bacon in half crosswise. Roll a half-slice of bacon around each date, tucking the loose end underneath to form a little package. If necessary, you can wrap the dates, then pierce them with a toothpick to hold the bacon in place. Arrange the dates, seam-side down, on the prepared baking sheet.

Put the baking sheet in the oven, then heat the oven to 400°F [200°C]. Bake for 10 minutes, then flip the dates and bake for another 5 to 15 minutes, or until the dates are golden brown and the bacon is crisp. Season with flaky salt and pepper. Serve hot!

TAHINI-DRIZZLED DATES

A SNACK FOR ONE OR MANY

If you think of a meal as a series of magical transformations, raw ingredients transmogrified into entirely new substances, then this—the mere application of tahini to date—is the equivalent of the first rabbit pulled out of a hat at a birthday party. You can dress up the dish with more fanfare in the form of salt flakes, spices, honey, and heat—the rabbit followed by flowers, then strings of colored cloth—but the essential magic rests in the combination of the two primary ingredients, which amp each other up to create something truly spectacular.

Dates

Tahini

This isn't really a recipe. Use as many big, squidgy dates as you like. You'll want at least two per person, maybe more. Pit the dates and flatten each one slightly to give the tahini more surface area to pool on. Lay out the dates on a platter, then spoon over liberal quantities of well-stirred tahini. Serve as is, or drizzle with honey, date molasses, and olive oil, then sprinkle with flaky salt, sesame seeds, rose petals, red pepper flakes, crushed pistachios . . .

GRILLED DATES IN GRAPEFRUIT & PAPRIKA OIL

12 DATES (MULTIPLIES EASILY)

Consider this a little something special to serve while loafing around at a barbecue, waiting for the main course to roll out. The recipe scales easily, so you can feed as many people as you need to. Put out toothpicks or cocktail picks so guests can fish out the dates and grapefruit chunks from the scented oil, and serve some bread alongside to mop up the juices.

If you don't have a grill, you can sear these on a gas stovetop, turning frequently, or put them under a broiler on high, flipping a few times. However you cook the dates, try to get them hot enough to give you a dramatic little sizzle when you slide them into the marinade.

I tested this recipe with toffee-sweet Lulu dates, but they can be hard to find outside the United Arab Emirates. Look for bite-size, relatively soft dates, such as Barhi or Sukkari, rather than jumbo Medjools or Deglet Nours.

1 to 3 garlic cloves

12 dates, pitted

12 unsalted, roasted almonds

3 Tbsp olive oil

1 tsp sweet smoked paprika

1 ruby red grapefruit

Salt

Freshly ground black pepper

Get your grill going until you have coals that are glowing but not aflame, warm enough that you can hover your hand over the coals for no more than 3 seconds.

Peel the garlic and cut it as thinly as you can. You want a single super-thin slice for each date, ideally so translucent you can read the newspaper through it. Stuff each date with one almond and one whisper of garlic, then thread the dates onto a skewer, piercing each date at an angle so that its seams are pinned shut. Thread 3 to 4 dates on each skewer.

In a large heatproof bowl, whisk together the olive oil and paprika. Halve the grapefruit, then use a grapefruit spoon or small sharp knife to chunk out the flesh and add it to the oil mixture. If possible, keep the pieces of grapefruit large enough for people to spear with their cocktail picks and eat. Squeeze in any juice left behind in the grapefruit halves. Whisk the mixture again, then season with salt and pepper—it should be tart and bitter from the grapefruit and the olive oil, and smoky from the paprika.

Grill the dates, turning the skewers every minute or so, for 3 to 5 minutes. Keep an eye on them: Dates are so high in sugar that they can burn quickly.

Carefully pull the dates off the skewers and immediately drop them into their oily grapefruit bath. The dates should still be hot enough that the oil sizzles briefly, which activates the flavors and encourages them to meld. Let the dates sit in the marinade for 15 minutes, then serve at room temperature.

CURRIED SAUSAGE ROLLS WITH A SURPRISE INSIDE

ABOUT 24 LITTLE BITES

The surprise—you guessed it—is dates. A long snake of date paste, to be exact, which is tucked into the center of these sausage rolls so that it seasons each bite all the way through. Serve with a fiery mustard alongside for added oomph.

8 oz [225 g] ground beef

1 yellow onion, finely diced

2 Tbsp curry powder of your choice

1 tsp salt (or less if your curry powder is salty)

1 tsp freshly ground black pepper

1 sheet (about 8 oz [225 g]) store-bought puff pastry, thawed following package instructions

1 cup [170 g] date paste

1 egg yolk, lightly beaten

1 Tbsp sesame seeds

Preheat the oven to 350°F [180°C]. Line a rimmed baking sheet with parchment paper.

In a large bowl, thoroughly combine the ground beef, onion, curry powder, salt, and pepper. Set aside.

Check your puff pastry to confirm that it is malleable but not sticky; if it's sticky, return it to the freezer for a few minutes. Use a rolling pin to roll it out between two sheets of parchment paper until about ⅛ in [3 mm] thick. Cut the puff pastry lengthwise into thirds so you have three long rectangles of dough.

Use your hands to roll the beef mixture into three sausage shapes, each about an inch [2.5 cm] in circumference, and center one lengthwise on each pastry rectangle. Leave enough clearance on the long sides for you to cover the beef completely with pastry, at least an inch [2.5 cm], if not more.

Channel your inner Play-Doh sculptor and roll the date paste into a very long, thin snake, about the width of a pencil. Cut the snake into thirds. Lay one third down the center of one of the ground beef sections, then bury it so that it's completely encased in the meat. Fold the pastry lengthways over the meat so that the filling is completely wrapped inside; seal the edges with a little bit of the egg yolk as needed.

Repeat with the remaining puff pastry, beef, and date paste to create three long rolls. Place the rolls on the prepared baking sheet and place in the freezer for 20 to 30 minutes, giving the mixture time to settle and making the rolls easier to slice.

Remove the rolls from the freezer and cut each one crosswise into 2 in [5 cm] long pieces. Place the sausage rolls on the baking sheet, then brush with the remaining egg yolk and sprinkle with the sesame seeds. Bake for 25 to 35 minutes, or until the meat is thoroughly cooked and the pastry is puffed and golden. Serve hot or at room temperature. Leftovers will keep in an airtight container in the refrigerator for 2 to 3 days; crisp up the pastry in a hot oven for 5 minutes if you don't enjoy a soggy roll.

TANDOORI-SPICED CANDIED PECANS

PRE-DINNER COCKTAIL SNACKS FOR 4

This is one of my favorite party snacks—there's something incredibly moreish about the sweet and salty combination set against the richness of the pecans. Serve these on their own, or as part of a cheese board. They're also delicious as the crunchy element of a special salad.

You will not need all of the masala mix for a single batch of pecans, but it's a handy and delicious seasoning for all kinds of food—Fish! Chicken! Tofu! Roasted vegetables!—and will keep in an airtight jar for several months. The nuts are also great with other spices subbed in: Try only cinnamon, or pumpkin spice, or just use a store-bought tandoori spice mix instead of making your own.

MASALA MIX

2 tsp ground cumin

2 tsp sweet smoked paprika

1 tsp garlic powder

1 tsp ground ginger

1 tsp ground coriander

1 tsp ground cardamom

1 tsp red chili powder (optional)

CANDIED PECANS

1 cup [120 g] pecan halves

2 Tbsp date molasses

1 tsp olive oil

Zest of 1 orange

Pinch of salt

Preheat the oven to 350°F [180°C]. Line a rimmed baking sheet with parchment paper.

TO MAKE THE MASALA MIX, in a small bowl, combine the cumin, paprika, garlic powder, ground ginger, coriander, cardamom, and red chili powder (if using).

TO MAKE THE CANDIED PECANS, in a small bowl filled with lukewarm water, soak the pecans for 10 minutes. Drain the pecans well, then toss them with the date molasses, olive oil, orange zest, salt, and 1 heaping tablespoon of the masala mix. Stir to combine.

Evenly spread the pecan mixture on the prepared baking sheet and bake until the date molasses is caramelized and bubbling, and it smells really good, 6 to 9 minutes.

Let cool on the baking sheet until the date molasses forms a thin shell around the nuts, about 20 minutes. Break into bite-size chunks and serve within the hour.

Note that the nuts won't stay crispy if you store them overnight—they get gooey but remain delicious despite the textural metamorphosis. The pecans keep for up to 5 days in an airtight container at room temperature.

HOT CHEESE DATES

ABOUT 50 BALLS

I can't count the number of times I've made this recipe. It's a riff on a retro-inflected Julia Reed joint for Hot Cheese Olives published in the *New York Times* in 2003 to accompany an article about "hostess" outfits.

Replacing the olives with dates turns these bites into the sort of passed app that has people strategically hovering in order to nab them from the tray before they hit the rest of the party. They are salty, sweet, crisp, soft: I make them for every special occasion. Serve on a silver platter with icy cold cocktails passed alongside.

If you're using larger dates, such as jumbo Medjools, slice them into thirds instead of halves. Use a box grater to grate the cheese yourself; don't buy pre-shredded—it isn't the same. These freeze well unbaked and are a very convenient item to have on hand for any spur-of-the-moment snacking. Place in a single layer on a baking sheet until frozen, then seal in a freezer-safe container for up to two months. Bake directly from frozen, adding on a few extra minutes of oven time.

½ cup [113 g] butter, at room temperature

8 oz [225 g] coarsely grated sharp Cheddar cheese (about 2 cups)

1½ cups [210 g] flour

2 Tbsp sesame seeds

1 tsp sweet smoked paprika

Big pinch of salt

1 large egg

15 to 25 dates, pitted

In a large bowl, beat the butter until creamy. Stir in the cheese until a wet paste forms. Add the flour, sesame seeds, paprika, and salt and stir until it reaches the texture of sand at the edge of the beach—a little moist and clumpy, a little dry. Some small lumps of butter are fine.

In a small bowl, whisk the egg with 2 tablespoons of water, then add to the dough mixture and knead until just blended. Refrigerate the dough for at least 30 minutes and up to overnight.

While the dough is resting, cut the dates in half and gently shape them into little balls about the size of an olive.

Preheat the oven to 350°F [180°C].

Take a piece of chilled dough about the size of a walnut and flatten it between your fingers into a thin disc. Place a date ball in the middle and shape and pinch the dough shut to enclose the date. Repeat with the remaining dough and dates, placing the balls on a baking sheet with about 1 in [2.5 cm] of space between them. Don't worry if the dough seems too crumbly; the heat of your fingers will warm up the butter and help bring it all together. Use the sides of your fingers, not just the tips, to coax the dough around the dates and roll gently between your palms to seal them shut. Patch up any holes with extra dough if needed.

Bake until the dough is matte and set, 15 to 20 minutes. Serve hot or at room temperature. Leftovers will keep, stored in an airtight container at room temperature, for up to 2 days.

DUCK & DATE JAM SANDOS

1 SANDWICH (MULTIPLIES EASILY)

Here are ingredients for one extremely rich sandwich: Scale up accordingly if desired. These go quickly at gatherings when they're sliced into fingers and set to circulate among your guests. Consider a teatime spread with these sandwiches, miniature versions of the Date & Cream Scones with Whipped Lemon-Vanilla Butter (page 94), a batch of the Lime & Ginger Crunch (page 200), and a big pot of tea.

You don't need duck rillettes for this recipe, really; you can substitute any sort of gamy and rich paté or potted meat spread you prefer. The recipe makes more pickled onion than needed for a single sandwich, but you might as well make a larger batch while you're at it—the onions are good on salads, as a topper for rice, and as a sneaky source of tang and color (that hot pink!) in any other sandwiches you might make for at least a week.

1 small red onion

¼ tsp salt

2 Tbsp red wine vinegar

2 thin slices brioche, crusts removed

About 2 Tbsp duck rillettes

1 Tbsp One-Ingredient Date Jam (page 238) or store-bought

Flaky salt

Freshly ground black pepper

Cut the onion lengthwise in half, then cut it into very thin half-moons. Place in a small nonreactive bowl and toss with the salt. Douse the onion slices liberally in red wine vinegar and allow to sit for at least 30 minutes and up to overnight. The onions are ready when they're light pink and yielding.

Toast both slices of brioche until just golden brown and crisp outside, tender within. (If you're making lots of these sandwiches, you can toast all the bread at once in a 300°F [150°C] oven).

Spread one slice of toast with the rillettes in a thick, even layer to cover the slice edge to edge. Lift 1 tablespoon of the red onion out of the pickling liquid, shake off excess moisture, and sprinkle over the rillettes. Slick the other slice of toast to cover with the date jam. Press the slices together into one very rich sandwich. Cut diagonally into quarters (or your preferred sandwich format). Season with salt and pepper. Serve on your nicest little plate accompanied by a glass of something very cold and dry.

DATE & KASHKAVAL GRILLED CHEESE

1 SANDWICH (MULTIPLIES EASILY)

This is barely a recipe. I'm basically just asking you to add dates to your regular grilled cheese situation and see how that makes you feel. If you can find it, Kashkaval is a mild yet unambiguously sheepy cheese from Bulgaria. It melts beautifully and it is the perfect foil to the sweet unctuousness of dates. Otherwise, any gentle melty cheese is good here. If you have ever had kunafa, the extravagant Palestinian dessert also known as "the king of sweets," you may notice a slight resemblance to the finished product: crunchy, salty, buttery, oozy, sweet. For a slightly more savory sandwich, try another kind of cheese: a sharp Cheddar, a mushroomy Brie, or a crumbly, chalky fresh goat cheese.

This sandwich is an ideal companion for a big bowl of soup. Consider serving it with the Double-Ginger Carrot Soup (page 150).

1 Tbsp butter
2 slices bread of your choice
2 to 4 slices Kashkaval cheese
1 or 2 dates, halved and pitted
Flaky salt
Freshly ground black pepper

In a medium skillet over medium-high heat, melt the butter until the foaming subsides. Place a slice of bread in the butter, then layer on the cheese and dates. Place the second slice of bread on top. Cook, pressing down with a spatula, until the bread on the bottom is a deep, even golden brown. Flip and cook until the second side matches the first. If the cheese isn't melting, cover the skillet to help things along. Season with salt and pepper. Enjoy right away.

TATER TOTS TOSSED IN HOT DATE! BUTTER

TOTS FOR 6 TO 8, DEPENDING ON HUNGER LEVELS AND AVAILABILITY OF OTHER SNACKS

Put these out at a gathering and I guarantee you'll be hearing rave reviews about your snack judgment for a long time to come. You'll need to make a batch of Hot Date! Butter (page 250) before you begin.

2 lbs [910 g] frozen tater tots

2 tsp garlic powder (optional)

5 Tbsp Hot Date! Butter (page 250), at room temperature

Salt

Freshly ground black pepper

Preheat the oven to 450°F [230°C].

In a large bowl, toss the tater tots with the garlic powder (if using), then spread the tots in a single layer on a baking sheet. Be sure to leave room for hot air to circulate around each tot—you may need two baking sheets to achieve this. Bake until the tots are deeply golden and crispy, 35 to 40 minutes (or follow the package instructions).

Just before the tots are done, in a small saucepan over low heat or the microwave, gently heat the butter until it begins to melt. Remove the cooked tots from the oven and transfer to a large bowl. Drizzle the butter over the tots and toss vigorously until they are thoroughly coated and smell delicious. Season with salt and pepper as needed. Serve warm. Have fun.

HERBACEOUS GARLIC BREAD

GARLIC BREAD FOR 4

For evenings when you need something
a little more refined than tater tots.

One recipe Hot Date! Butter (page 250)
1 fresh baguette

Preheat the oven to 400°F [200°C].
 Hasselback your baguette by
cutting deep crosswise slits but not
cutting all the way through—leave
each slice connected at the bottom.
Smear a generous amount of the
butter between each of the slices.
Wrap the baguette in aluminum foil
and place on a baking sheet, seam-
side up. Bake for 15 minutes, then
unwrap the foil from the top and bake,
exposed, until crisp, another 3 to
5 minutes. Serve hot and encourage
your guests to rend the loaf asunder.

"ANTS ON A LOG"

SNACKS FOR 4

A primo snack, given a little nudge to break it away from peanut butter's iron grip. Whipping tahini with cold water fluffs it up and gives it a loose, silky texture; if you refrigerate it for several hours, it will firm up into a dense mousse that retains its shape when sliced or spooned. Both versions taste great with celery and dates.

1 cup [260 g] tahini
¼ cup [60 ml] fresh lemon juice
1½ tsp salt
10 to 12 large, squishy dates, such as Medjools
1 head celery, washed and cut into finger lengths

In a food processor, blend the tahini, lemon juice, and salt. With the food processor running, gradually stream in 1 cup [240 ml] of cold water until the mixture becomes pale and creamy. Don't worry if it breaks—this is a normal part of the process, and it will come back together again. Keep slowly drizzling in water until the whipped tahini holds a soft peak. Taste and season with salt if needed.

Halve and pit the dates, then cut each half lengthwise into quarters. Use a teaspoon or offset spatula to fill each rib of celery with whipped tahini, then stud with date slices. Equally enjoyable as an after-school snack or a nostalgic bit of finger food at a party. These are best enjoyed within an hour or two of assembly, but you can whip the tahini ahead of time and store it overnight before filling the celery spears.

CRISPY SAUTÉED DATES ON A SAFFRON CLOUD

This dish is a messy pleasure. Encourage your guests to eat with their hands and provide a generous stack of napkins for the wiping of sticky fingers.

Big pinch of saffron (about 15 threads)

1½ cups [375 g] fresh whole-milk ricotta cheese, at room temperature

Zest of ½ lemon (about 1 tsp)

¼ cup [60 ml] olive oil

12 dates, pitted and halved

One 9 x 13 in [23 x 33 cm] slab fresh, crunchy, oily focaccia

Pinch of smoked red chili flakes (optional)

Flaky salt

Freshly ground black pepper

In a medium bowl, steep the saffron threads in 2 tablespoons of warm water until the liquid turns the color of the sun, 15 to 20 minutes. Add the ricotta and lemon zest and whisk until you have a smooth, fluffy mixture. Set aside.

In a medium skillet over medium heat, warm the olive oil. Place the dates, cut-side down, in the skillet and cook, turning a few times, until they start to caramelize and are just heated through, 3 to 4 minutes. Be careful—they burn easily.

Arrange the focaccia on a serving platter and spread with a thick layer of the ricotta, as though you are frosting a cake with generous abandon. Tumble the dates and their infused oil over the ricotta cloud, then sprinkle with the smoked red chili flakes (if using), enough salt that it is unmistakably salty, and pepper. Place within easy reach of your guests and let them tear in. Once assembled, this doesn't make for great leftovers—everything gets a bit soggy—so encourage everyone to eat up.

SESAME-CRUSTED HALLOUMI

Golden Halloumi, garlicky date molasses, and a sprightly tuxedo of black and white sesame seeds: What more could you ask for? For variations on the same theme, swap some Burnt Date Honey (page 252) for the garlic-infused molasses in the recipe, use just one color of sesame seed, or throw in some nigella seeds instead.

3 garlic cloves

1 cup [240 ml] date molasses

2 Tbsp toasted white sesame seeds

2 Tbsp toasted black sesame seeds

8 oz [225 g] plain Halloumi cheese, drained and patted dry

2 Tbsp olive oil

Flaky salt

Start the recipe a couple of hours before you intend to eat. Use the flat of your knife to crush each garlic clove, then remove the peel (it should come away easily). Tip the crushed cloves into a small jar, then cover with the date molasses. Set aside in a cool place to let the flavors mingle properly, at least 2 hours and up to overnight. Remove the garlic before using.

Combine the black and white sesame seeds in a saucer and set aside.

Cut the Halloumi into planks or triangles, each about ½ in [13 mm] thick. In a large skillet over medium-high heat, warm the olive oil until shimmering. Arrange the Halloumi in a single layer, being sure to leave ample space around each piece. Depending on the size of your skillet, you may need to cook the cheese in batches. Cook for just 1 to 2 minutes per side, or until a golden crust forms, then flip and cook the other side. Remove from the heat and brush each piece of Halloumi with a generous amount of the garlic-infused date molasses. Roll each piece in the sesame seeds until thickly coated. Arrange the Halloumi on a serving platter and hit with a pinch of salt and maybe another little drizzle of infused date molasses. Serve warm.

BAKED CAMEMBERT

CHEESE FOR 6 TO 8, AS PART OF A LARGER SPREAD, OR AN APPETIZER FOR 4

I almost titled this entire chapter "Dates & Dairy: A Love Story," because there are just so many excellent date and cheese combinations. Behold! A symphony of melty cheese, fiery garlic, and sweet date.

1 wheel Camembert or Brie, preferably in a little wooden case

1 Medjool or 2 smaller dates, thinly sliced

1 garlic clove, grated with a Microplane or very finely minced

Splash of olive oil

Pinch of salt

Flatbread, pita chips, or crackers, for serving

Preheat the oven to 350°F [180°C].
Unwrap any paper or plastic coverings from the cheese and discard. Using a small sharp knife, cut a pattern of crosshatched shallow lines across the top of the cheese. Place the cheese back in its wooden case and plop it onto a baking sheet. If your cheese didn't come in a case, put it directly on the baking sheet.

In a small bowl, use your fingers or a fork to mash together the date, garlic, olive oil, and salt. Slather this mixture on top of the cheese, working it into the grooves you cut. Slide the cheese into the oven for 10 to 15 minutes, or until it is melty and you can smell the garlic. Serve right away with warm flatbread, pita chips, or crackers.

MUSK-SCENTED DATE FRITTERS

PIT DATES. TAKE BLANCHED, PEELED & GROUND PISTACHIOS, & MAKE IT INTO A PASTE WITH SUGAR, ROSE WATER & MUSK. USE TO STUFF the DATES. TAKE CREPE BATTER [...] DIP the DATES INTO the BATTER, FRY IN SESAME OIL, & PUT INTO THICK SYRUP. [REPEAT]. THEN ARRANGE ON A PLATE, SPRINKLE WITH SUGAR & PISTACHIOS, & SPRAY WITH ROSE WATER and MUSK.

FROM «كتاب الوصلة إلى الحبيب في وصف الطيبات والطيب» TRANSLATED INTO ENGLISH AS "SCENTS AND FLAVORS the BANQUETER SAVORS: A SYRIAN COOKBOOK" BY CHARLES PERRY (NYU PRESS 2020). THIS ANONYMOUSLY WRITTEN THIRTEENTH-CENTURY COOKBOOK WAS A POPULAR TEXT, ORGANIZED ROUGHLY IN PARALLEL WITH the STAGES of a BANQUET. DERIVED FROM THE GLAND of a TUSKED DEER, MUSK WAS USED EXTENSIVELY IN MEDIEVAL MIDDLE EASTERN TIMES. A UBIQUITOUS INGREDIENT IN PERFUMES, IT WAS ALSO ADDED to FOOD and DRINK for its AROMATIC and ANTI-DECAYING PROPERTIES.

CHOCOLATE, DATE & OLIVE OIL TOASTS

A MOUTHFUL FOR 12 (MULTIPLIES EASILY)

All the pleasure of a pain au chocolat, none of the hard work. The contrast of the bitter olive oil and just-warm dark chocolate against the sweet date, the crunchy salt, and the soft bread deliver an entire universe in a single bite: peak party food, a lovely mouthful to pass around at any point in the proceedings.

This melange was inspired by an Amanda Hesser recipe in the *New York Times* that I've kept in my back pocket for the last twenty-odd years, ready to unleash upon any last-minute gathering. Prep everything while your oven heats, plop it in just long enough for the flavors to come together, and you're feeding people in fifteen minutes.

3 large soft dates, such as Medjools

1 fresh baguette, cut into 12 thin slices

12 thin pieces very good dark chocolate, each about 1 in [2.5 cm] square

Your best extra-virgin olive oil

Flaky sea salt, like Maldon

Preheat the oven to 350°F [180°C].

Cut the dates lengthwise in half, then in half again to give you four long pieces per date.

Arrange the baguette slices in a single layer on a baking sheet. Top each slice with a piece of chocolate and a slice of date. Drizzle each piece with a little olive oil and sprinkle with a few flakes of salt. Slide the baking sheet into the oven for just a few minutes, until the chocolate starts to lose its sharp edges and begins to slump but is not actually melting, and the dates are warm but not hot. This should take no longer than 5 minutes, probably less. Remove from the oven and transfer to a serving platter, then up the ante with a fresh application of olive oil and salt. Serve right away.

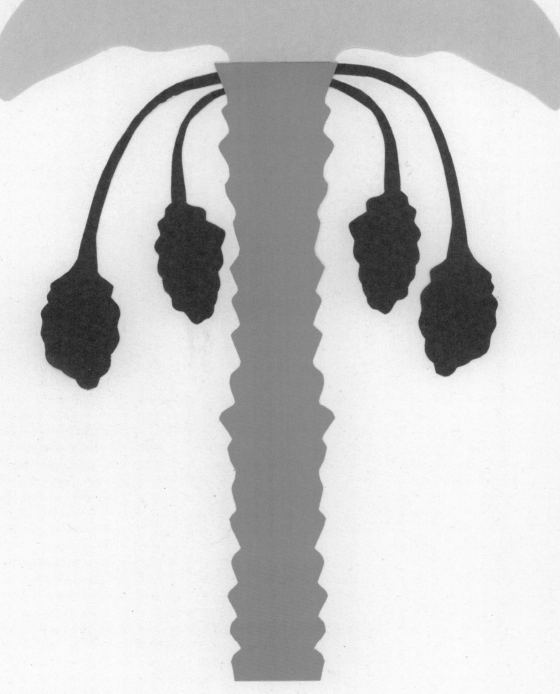

DATE & TAHINI GRANOLA

ABOUT 7 CUPS [1 KG]

This is our house granola, because it is both delicious and adaptable. Swap out the nuts, sub in seeds, mix in whatever dried fruit you want. I've even made it with maple syrup instead of date molasses. But this is the version we like best. The date molasses and tahini swathe each morsel in an addictive, salty-sweet coating that is hard to stop snacking on. We spoon this granola onto yogurt, use it to top fruit crumbles, layer it in parfaits, and eat it out of hand throughout the day.

If you like your granola on the chewy side, bake it for less time (35 to 45 minutes) and pack it more tightly in the baking sheet; for crispier granola, bake it longer (40 to 50 minutes) and spread it out in a thinner, more even layer. As always, much depends on your individual oven.

2 cups [200 g] old-fashioned rolled oats (not quick-cooking or instant)

1 cup [140 g] raw unsalted pistachios, left whole or coarsely chopped

1 cup [120 g] raw unsalted walnut halves, left whole or coarsely chopped

1 cup [100 g] unsweetened coconut flakes

⅔ cup [160 ml] date molasses

½ cup [100 g] packed light brown sugar

½ cup [120 ml] olive oil

⅓ cup [80 g] tahini

1 tsp salt

1 cup [175 g] chopped dates

Preheat the oven to 300°F [150°C]. Line a rimmed baking sheet with parchment paper.

In a large bowl, combine the oats, pistachios, walnuts, coconut flakes, date molasses, brown sugar, olive oil, tahini, and salt and stir until everything is thoroughly coated and a little wet and shiny.

Spread your granola mixture evenly on the prepared baking sheet. Bake, stirring every 10 to 15 minutes, anywhere from 35 to 50 minutes total, depending on how chewy versus crispy you want your granola. The granola should be fragrant and toasted by the time you're ready to pull it out of the oven.

Let the granola cool on the baking sheet on a wire rack before stirring in the chopped dates and seasoning with more salt as needed. Leftovers will keep, stored in a jar or other airtight container at room temperature, for up to a month.

DATES

① OLIVE OIL   ② ZA'ATAR

DIP BREAD in ① then ②. EAT & REPEAT!

SHAMI BREAKFAST—
AN INCOMPLETE ACCOUNTING, EMPHATICALLY NOT to SCALE, of the BEST WAY to START the DAY

SAUCERS of JAM & FRESH ASHTA, or CLOTTED CREAM

LABNEH & OLIVE OIL

FUL M'DAMMAS

PICKLED BABY EGGPLANTS

HUMMUS

MANY FRESH CRUNCHY VEGETABLES

WATERMELON!   (WHEN in SEASON)

CHEESE PARADE

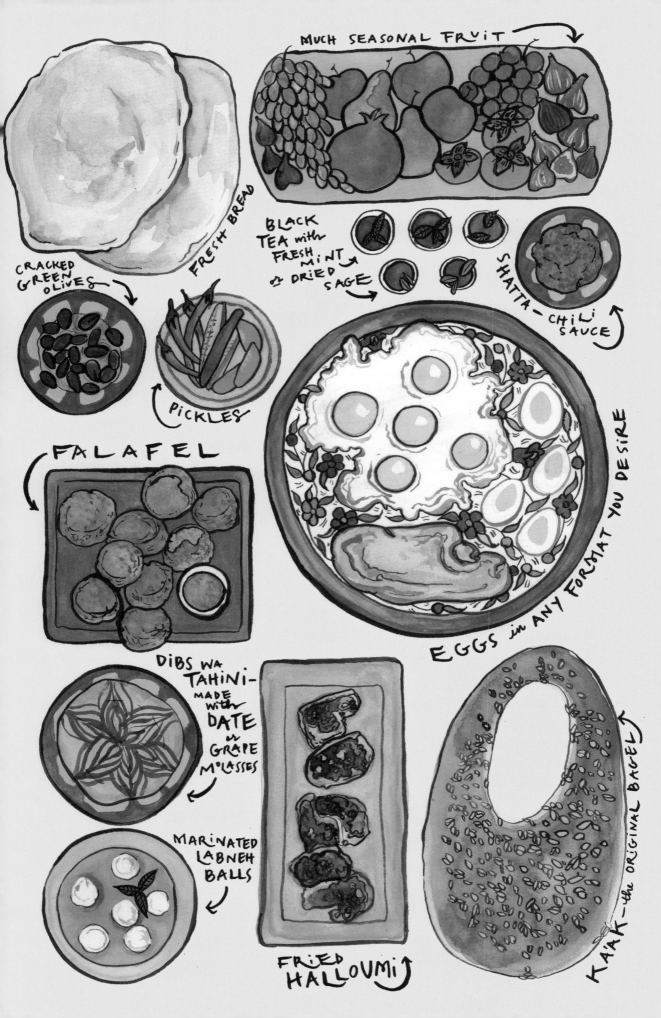

MUCH SEASONAL FRUIT

FRESH BREAD

CRACKED GREEN OLIVES

BLACK TEA with FRESH MINT & DRIED SAGE

SHATTA — CHILI SAUCE

PICKLES

FALAFEL

EGGS in ANY FORMAT YOU DESiRE

DIBS WA TAHINI — MADE with DATE or GRAPE MOLASSES

MARINATED LABNEH BALLS

FRIED HALLOUMI

KA'AK — the ORIGINAL BAGEL

DIBS WA TAHINI

A recipe that is barely a recipe. In a shallow saucer, pour out a glug of well-stirred tahini. Use a fork or teaspoon to drizzle date molasses on top of the tahini. The proportions are up to you; consider whether you like your PB&J more weighted towards peanut butter or jam and act accordingly. Warm up a fresh pita, tear off a piece, dip, and eat. This is a classic breakfast dish served across the Middle East, sometimes with carob molasses or grape molasses instead of the date version.

I AM A STALWART
WHO CLEARS ALL HURDLES
in the FRAY
FOR the SAKE of BELLES DRESSED
in GORGEOUS ROBES;
The GLITTER of TEETH LiKE
DAZZLING WHITE PALM POLLEN.

—Al-Mayidi Ibn Zahir

... THE GLiTTER of TEETH LiKE DAZZLiNG WHiTE PALM POLLEN...

SCULPTURAL BREAKFAST BARS

ABOUT 20 BARS

There's something magical about this particular no-bake combination of nuts and dried fruit, held together by a sticky lattice of date paste. It's a rich and fragrant little arrangement to wrap up for later and pull out when you need breakfast or a burst of energy. You can, of course, experiment with not just the nuts and dried fruit you use, but also the shapes you make—try balls, logs, cubes, or whatever sculptural forms the breakfast muse dictates.

1 cup [120 g] raw or roasted unsalted hazelnuts

1 cup [120 g] raw or roasted unsalted walnut halves

1 cup [180 g] dried apricots

1 cup [120 g] dried mango

1 cup [175 g] date paste

1 vanilla bean or 1 tsp vanilla extract (optional)

Zest of 1 lime

1 cup [20 g] puffed rice and/or puffed quinoa

Line a rimmed quarter baking sheet with two strips of parchment paper crisscrossed to form a sling. Finely chop the hazelnuts and walnuts. You can do this with a knife (very satisfying), or use a food processor or mortar and pestle to crush them into coarse crumbs.

Finely chop the apricots and mango by hand or using a food processor. You want them to retain some texture and not turn into a paste.

In a large bowl, combine the nuts, dried fruit, and date paste, then use your hands to thoroughly combine the mixture, kneading it if needed.

If using the vanilla bean, use a small sharp knife to cut it lengthwise in half, then use the back of the knife to scrape the seeds from inside the bean directly into the bowl with the nut and fruit mixture. Alternatively, add the vanilla extract. Stir in the lime zest, then add the puffed rice or quinoa and gently stir to work it into the mixture

Press the mixture firmly into the prepared baking sheet. The bars should be at least ½ in [13 mm] thick. Refrigerate for at least 30 minutes, then use the overhanging parchment to turn out onto a chopping board and cut into even bars. Eat as is or crumble on top of yogurt. Leftovers will keep, in an airtight container in the refrigerator, for up to 1 week, or in the freezer for up to 2 months.

PUMPKIN PANCAKES WITH WARM RAS EL HANOUT SYRUP

BREAKFAST FOR 4

Chebab, spiced pancakes drizzled with date molasses, are a traditional breakfast dish from the United Arab Emirates. This recipe messes around with that basic notion, adding a big dose of rich pumpkin purée. Dates and winter squash make very cozy companions, and these pancakes are an ideal showcase for their complementary properties. With their robust, complex sweetness, both can stand up to assertive spice blends. I like to use ras el hanout, which translates to "top of the shop" and is a Moroccan spice blend that varies wildly from maker to maker. If you can't find it, consider another warm and fragrant blend, such as powdered chai spices, pumpkin spice, or even a teaspoon each of ground cinnamon and ginger. Whatever you choose, make sure you layer in the spices so they can build on each other, using the same blend in the pancake batter and in the date syrup.

Cook these lower and slower than you would regular pancakes; the pumpkin takes longer to cook through and is prone to burning at high heat. You do, however, want the heat high enough for the pancakes to develop deeply golden brown, crispy exteriors that are just shy of burnt for maximum textural contrast and joyous flavor. Cooking the pancakes in ghee instead of butter will help you achieve this, due to ghee's richness and higher smoke point.

SPICED DATE SYRUP

½ cup [120 ml] date molasses

1 Tbsp butter or ghee

1 tsp ras el hanout

1 tsp almond extract (optional)

PUMPKIN PANCAKES

1½ cups [210 g] plus 1 tsp flour

2 Tbsp sugar

2 tsp ras el hanout

1 tsp baking powder

1 tsp baking soda

1 tsp salt

1½ cups [360 ml] buttermilk

¾ cup [170 g] pumpkin purée

1 egg

3 Tbsp melted ghee, plus more for the skillet

1 tsp vanilla extract

¾ cup [110 g] chopped dates

Salted butter and chopped pecans, for serving

TO MAKE THE SPICED DATE SYRUP, in a small saucepan over medium-low heat, combine the date molasses, butter, ras el hanout, and almond extract. Gently warm, stirring until the butter is just melted and the mixture is glossy and fragrant. Set aside.

TO MAKE THE PUMPKIN PANCAKES, in a large bowl, whisk together the 1½ cups [210 g] of flour, the sugar, ras el hanout, baking powder, baking soda, and salt.

In a medium bowl, whisk together the buttermilk, pumpkin purée, egg, ghee, and vanilla until fully combined and smooth. Add to the flour mixture and mix until just combined.

In a small bowl, toss the dates with the remaining 1 teaspoon of flour to coat, then add the dates to the batter and very gently fold just enough to evenly distribute them.

Heat a medium skillet or pancake griddle over medium-low heat, then pour in a goodly quantity of ghee—you want about ⅛ in [3 mm] of ghee covering the bottom of the skillet. Once the ghee is properly hot, working in batches, drop in your pancake batter by about ¼ cup at a time, leaving room between the pancakes for them to spread out. Cook the pancakes until their tops begin to bubble and their edges look golden brown and crispy, 2 to 3 minutes, then flip the pancakes and cook until the other sides are similarly dark golden and crispy and the pancakes are puffy and cooked through their centers. Continue cooking more pancakes with the remaining batter, adding

CONT'D

more ghee to the pan as needed
between batches. Serve hot with
lashings of spiced date syrup, salted
butter, and a shower of chopped
pecans. Pancakes can be made ahead
and frozen in a single layer on a baking sheet; remove once fully frozen
and store in an airtight container or
bag for up to 2 months. Reheat in the
oven or a toaster. Any leftover syrup
can be decanted into a little jar and
refrigerated for up to a week—it is
wonderful mixed into a hot toddy or
a mug of hot milk if you need another
use for it.

POMEGRANATE PARFAITS

PARFAITS FOR 4

Marinating pomegranate seeds in date molasses and orange blossom water adds depth and nuance to the tartness of the fruit. You can make a stunner of a centerpiece by layering this in a glass bowl and dishing it up trifle-style for a large-format breakfast; if you do this, you will need to supplement with more pomegranates or other red fruit, such as strawberries or raspberries, or veer even more tart with blood orange segments.

One of life's great pleasures is a small spoonful of marinated pomegranate seeds dropped into a coupe of champagne. Cheers!

2 Tbsp date molasses

1 tsp orange blossom water

Seeds from 1 pomegranate

2 cups [480 g] full-fat plain yogurt

Zest of 1 orange (about 1 Tbsp), plus more for garnish

1 cup [115 g] granola of your choice (store-bought or Date & Tahini Granola, page 74)

In a small bowl, combine 1 tablespoon of the date molasses, the orange blossom water, and the pomegranate seeds. Cover and refrigerate for at least 1 hour and up to 24 hours.

To assemble your parfaits, in a medium bowl, combine the yogurt, orange zest, and the remaining 1 tablespoon of date molasses. In four separate glasses, spoon in alternating layers of the pomegranate seeds and their juices, yogurt, and granola. Begin and end with the pomegranates, so they're at the top of the glass and all the way at the bottom. You should use about ½ cup [115 g] of yogurt and ¼ cup [30 g] of granola per serving. Top with jaunty curlicues of orange zest. Serve right away if you like your granola crunchy; otherwise, these parfaits will keep in the refrigerator for up to 24 hours.

HALWA-STUFFED FRENCH TOAST

BREAKFAST FOR 4

French toast with a hidden treat in the center—what's not to love? Date paste and halwa make a fragrant and satisfying filling for the extra-thick slices of bread. Leave the bread out overnight to turn stale if possible; it's easier to stuff and greatly improves the finished texture of the dish.

The mastic is optional but really adds wow factor. For more on mastic, see the Hot Date! Pantry (page 38).

8 thick slices brioche, challah, or tsoureki, each at least 1¼ in [3 cm] thick and ideally left to turn stale overnight

¼ cup [65 g] tahini

¾ cup [180 ml] whole milk

3 eggs

½ tsp vanilla extract

½ tsp ground cinnamon

¼ tsp salt

1 or 2 pebbles mastic (¼ tsp) (optional)

8 Tbsp [90 g] date paste

8 Tbsp [120 g] halwa, in large crumbles

Oil or butter, for cooking

Fresh fruit (bananas are nice here), maple syrup or date molasses for extra sweetness, pats of salted butter, a swoosh of labneh or Greek yogurt, confectioners' sugar, mint sprigs, a sprinkling of lavender sugar . . . Think the usual French toast accoutrements, for serving

Make a slit in the top crust of each slice of bread, like the coin slot in a piggy bank. You want each slice of bread to open like a pita pocket, so it's connected on three sides but open partially at the top. If you find this annoyingly fiddly, you can use two thinner slices of bread for each "piece" of French toast—I just find it much easier to flip the pieces if they're assembled like this. Note that stale bread will be much easier to wrangle than fresh.

In a large, shallow bowl, stir the tahini until smooth, then whisk in the milk, eggs, vanilla, cinnamon, and salt. If using mastic, crush the pebbles in a mortar and pestle into a fine powder, then add to your eggy mixture. Whisk until thoroughly combined and there are no large streaks of egg.

Carefully stuff about a tablespoon of date paste and a tablespoon of halwa into each slice of bread, spreading them thickly without smooshing the bread too much. If your halwa is very crumbly, mix it into the date paste first, then stuff the bread.

In a large skillet over medium heat, warm the oil or butter. Dunk the slices of stuffed bread into the egg mixture and soak for 15 to 30 seconds per side, until they've absorbed some egginess. Don't leave them in too long or they'll get too soggy and fall apart. Working in batches, add the stuffed and soaked bread to the skillet and cook until golden, 3 to 4 minutes per side. Repeat with the remaining bread, adding more oil or butter to the pan between batches as needed. Serve warm with any or all of the suggested toppings. This does not make for great leftovers, so enjoy right away.

DRAGON FRUIT & CARDAMOM SMOOTHIES

2 LARGE SMOOTHIES

This makes the hottest hot pink drink, a treat for the eyes and a beautiful way to start the morning. It's probably also the smoothie I make the most often at home. There's something particularly enchanting about the way the flavors play together, with the sweetness of the dates and the coconut water harmonizing with the tropical fruit. The cardamom is optional but highly encouraged—it adds an ethereal note that takes this from an everyday breakfast smoothie to something quite special.

2 large or 3 smaller dates

1 large ripe fresh or frozen banana

1 cup [110 g] frozen pink dragon fruit (pitaya)

1 cup [240 ml] coconut water

1 cup [240 ml] milk of your choice (I like whole milk or unsweetened almond milk)

Seeds from 2 green cardamom pods or ¼ tsp ground cardamom

In a high-powered blender, combine the dates, banana, dragon fruit, coconut water, milk, and cardamom Blend until smooth and frothy. Serve icy cold.

BUTTERFRUIT LASSIS

2 LARGE LASSIS

Avocados are also called butterfruit in India—an evocative name that speaks to the lush richness they lend this bright green lassi. They grow prolifically in certain parts of the subcontinent and are often used to spin up a cooling beverage. Dates aren't a traditional inclusion, but I prefer their earthy candor to sugar's one-note sweetness.

1 large or 2 small fully ripe avocados, roughly chopped

3 large or 5 small dates, pitted and roughly chopped

1 cup [240 ml] whole milk

¾ cup [170 g] full-fat plain yogurt

2 tsp rosewater

Seeds from 2 green cardamom pods or ¼ tsp ground cardamom

In a high-powered blender, combine the avocados, dates, milk, yogurt, rosewater, and cardamom. Blend until limpid green and very smooth and creamy. Refrigerate if needed and serve cold cold cold.

MOROCCAN AVOCADO SMOOTHIES

2 SUBSTANTIAL SMOOTHIES

While this Moroccan combination is a sunset standby during Ramadan, it's just as delicious and satisfying at the start of the day. The almond is meant to make its presence felt rather than dissolve into the background—if you have almond meal or almond extract on hand, please use them! The orange blossom water is optional but, as ever, highly encouraged.

2 cups [475 ml] unsweetened almond milk

1 large or 2 small fully ripe avocados, roughly chopped

6 dates, pitted and roughly chopped

2 Tbsp almond meal or ¼ tsp almond extract (optional)

1 tsp orange blossom water (optional)

1 cup [175 g] ice (optional)

In a high-powered blender, combine the almond milk, avocados, dates, almond meal or extract (if using), orange blossom water (if using), and ice (if using). Blend until smooth and creamy. Refrigerate if needed and serve icy cold.

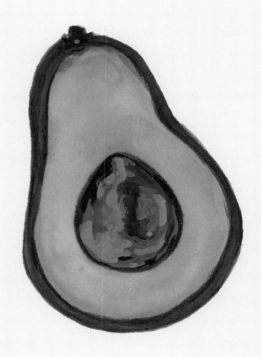

FOODS ARE SYMBOLS THAT WE CONSUME, and the DATE IS A PARTICULARLY POTENT ONE. DURING RAMADAN, the HOLY MONTH of FASTING (AND FEASTING!) OBSERVED BY PRACTICING MUSLIMS AROUND the WORLD, the DATE ACQUIRES EVEN MORE METAPHORIC WEIGHT. WE FAST FROM SUNRISE to SUNSET for an ENTIRE LUNAR MONTH, WATCHING the MOON WAX from FRAGILE CRESCENT to FULL ORB to NEW MOON AGAIN, NARROWING OUR FOCUS to EID AL FITR, the FESTIVAL MARKING the END of the FAST. IN THIS CONTEXT, DATES ARE SYMBOLS of ANTICIPATION RECIPROCITY GENEROSITY ABUNDANCE. THEY TRANSCEND SPACE and TIME.

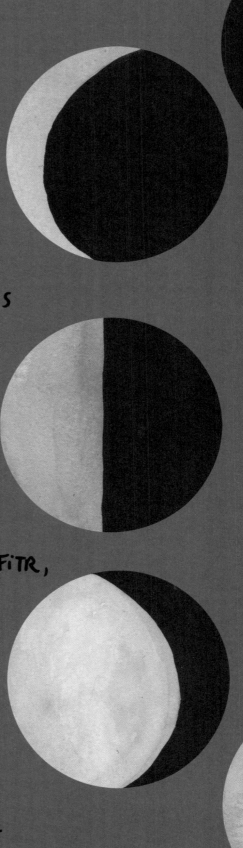

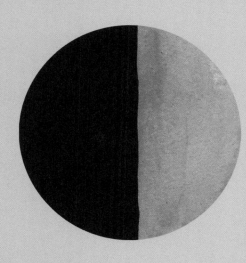

AT the MOMENT of
SUNSET, PEOPLE ACROSS
the GLOBE EAT A
DATE to BREAK
THEIR FASTS. IT is ONE
of the MOST PROFOUND
FOOD-BASED BONDS in
EXISTENCE, A RITUALIZED
POINT of CONNECTION, A
SIMULTANEITY RIPPLING
FROM ONE TIMEZONE to
the NEXT—THE SUN SETS,
the CALL to PRAYER BEGINS,
SIGHS of RELIEF and
BLESSINGS UPON the FOOD
ARE UTTERED, and the
NEARLY 2 BILLION PEOPLE
WHO OBSERVE RAMADAN TAKE
THEIR FIRST SIP of WATER
SINCE DAWN—and, MORE
OFTEN THAN NOT, EAT A
DATE, EMULATING the
PROPHET MUHAMMAD.

GHISAVA, OR CUPID'S OMELET

BREAKFAST FOR 2

A date . . . omelet? Before I cooked it, I found it hard to imagine what this dish, which is eaten in the chilly Azeri-speaking provinces of Iran, would taste like. But after one bite, its appeal was clear: It has the same salty-sweet eggy satisfaction as French toast and makes a lovely and sustaining breakfast on a cold morning. In her book *Dates: A Global History*, Iraqi historian Nawal Nasrallah details a very similar version of this dish, which she calls "Cupid's Omelet," with a wink and a nod towards its supposed aphrodisiac qualities. Do what you will with that information.

I tested this recipe using unbelievably delicious dark and silky Mazafati dates from the ancient Iranian city of Bam. I highly recommend tracking them down if you can—see the Where to Shop section (page 260) for advice on where to order some in the United States.

A more traditional version of this dish is even faster and easier: Roughly chop the dates and sauté in butter, then pour in the beaten eggs and scramble gently until just set. Whatever technique you choose, it makes for a hearty and comforting yet intriguing breakfast accompanied by a cup of sweet black tea with fresh mint or cardamom, and some warm pita or lavash alongside.

12 small or 6 large dates

5 eggs

½ tsp salt

½ tsp ground cinnamon, plus more for serving

½ tsp ground ginger (optional)

2 Tbsp butter

¼ cup [30 g] raw walnut halves, roughly chopped (optional)

Warm pita or lavash, for serving

Heat the broiler on low.

Cut each date lengthwise in half and remove the pits.

In a medium bowl, whisk together the eggs, salt, cinnamon, and ginger (if using).

In an ovenproof skillet over medium-low heat, melt 1 tablespoon of the butter until it foams. Add the dates, cut-side down, and sauté until they are slightly softened and you can smell them starting to caramelize. The dates can burn quite quickly, so keep an eye on them! Remove the dates from the pan and set aside.

Add the remaining 1 tablespoon of butter to the skillet, then tip in the walnuts (if using) and cook, stirring, until you can just start to smell them toasting, 1 to 2 minutes. Pour in the eggs and scramble gently for 1 to 2 minutes. Remove from the heat while the eggs are still quite runny,

then place the dates, cut-side down, in a circular pattern in the eggs. Put the eggs under the broiler for 1 minute, then start to check them for doneness every minute moving forward. The omelet is ready when the tops of the eggs have firmed slightly and puffed up around the date halves, and the domes of the dates are nicely caramelized. Dust some more cinnamon on top before serving warm or at room temperature with warm pita.

DATE & CREAM SCONES WITH WHIPPED LEMON-VANILLA BUTTER

8 SCONES

These are the scones I make on a lazy weekend morning when I want to feel like I've baked without actually putting any effort into the endeavor. They come together in a single bowl and are always light and fluffy: a tender, date-laden dream. The lemon-vanilla butter is a nice touch for days when you're feeling particularly luxurious—these scones make a luscious teatime snack served with a pot of tea and a spread of little sandwiches.

SCONES

2 cups [280 g] flour

½ cup [100 g] sugar

1 Tbsp baking powder

1 tsp salt

1½ cups [360 ml] heavy cream

1 cup [150 g] dates, pitted and roughly chopped

LEMON-VANILLA BUTTER

½ cup [113 g] butter, at room temperature

1 vanilla bean

Zest of 1 lemon (about 2 tsp)

1 Tbsp fresh lemon juice

¼ tsp salt

TO MAKE THE SCONES, preheat the oven to 400°F [200°C].

In a large bowl, use a fork to stir together the flour, sugar, baking powder, and salt. Make a well in the center, then pour in the heavy cream and stir until just combined. Stir in the dates. You want as light a touch as possible here—the less you work the dough, the more tender the scones will be.

Eyeball around eight similarly sized portions of dough and use a large spoon to drop them onto a baking sheet with 2 in [5 cm] of clearance around each one. Bake until pale golden and fragrant, 12 to 15 minutes.

Meanwhile, **TO MAKE THE LEMON-VANILLA BUTTER**, put the butter in a medium bowl. Use a small sharp knife to cut the vanilla bean lengthwise in half, then use the back of the knife to scrape the seeds from inside the bean directly into the bowl. Add the lemon zest, lemon juice, and salt. Whisk until the butter is smooth and visibly lightened. Serve with the hot scones while the butter is still room temperature for optimal slathering.

The scones are best consumed the day they're made but can be stored in an airtight container on the counter and revived the next day with a few minutes in a hot oven. The butter will keep, tightly covered in the refrigerator, for up to 3 days.

EGGY BREAKFAST SANDWICHES WITH DATE & OLIVE TAPENADE

4 SANDWICHES

This is a savory, yolky, messy sandwich for mornings that require sustenance with substance. I used Ajwa dates in the tapenade because they are assertive enough to stand up to the kalamata olives in terms of both color and taste. You can, of course, use whatever dates you like. The tapenade also makes a great marinade for meat (toss a couple of lamb chops in it, tenderize overnight, and then grill), as well as the base for a robust salad dressing—thin it out with a little more oil, then massage vigorously into finely shredded kale, cabbage, or collard greens.

TAPENADE

4 dates, pitted and minced

10 kalamata olives, pitted and minced

¼ cup [60 ml] olive brine

¼ cup [60 ml] olive oil

2 garlic cloves, minced

1 Tbsp mustard

SANDWICHES

1 Tbsp olive oil, plus more for the eggs

1 poblano or green bell pepper, cut into ½ in [13 mm] thick slices

1 large red onion, cut into ½ in [13 mm] thick rings

4 eggs

Salt

4 soft buns, preferably brioche, sliced in half

4 oz [115 g] sharp Cheddar cheese, cut into 4 thick slices

TO MAKE THE TAPENADE, in a medium bowl combine the dates, olives, olive brine, olive oil, garlic, and mustard, giving it all a good stir. Set aside to let the flavors mingle.

TO MAKE THE SANDWICHES, in a large skillet over medium-high heat, warm the olive oil. Add the pepper and red onion, and cook, stirring frequently, until they soften and darken and are nice and fragrant, about 5 minutes. Set the pepper and onion aside, then wipe the pan clean and return to medium-high heat.

Add a bit more oil if needed and fry the eggs until the whites are set but the yolks are still runny. Hit the eggs with a generous pinch of salt while still in the pan.

Meanwhile, toast the buns.

To assemble, top the bottom of each bun with a generous dollop of tapenade, a tangle of onions and peppers, a thick slice of cheese (you can melt it if you prefer but I like the crumbly texture of a nice sharp Cheddar here), and a fried egg to crown it all. Pop on the top bun and smoosh down so the yolk runs over everything and dresses it just so. Good morning!

BACON BREAKFAST SANDWICHES WITH SPICED DATE CHILI CRISP

4 SANDWICHES

Sometimes, your morning needs to begin with a remedy. On those days, a bacon sandwich—in all of its salty, fatty, bready glory—is necessary. Add the elusive sweetness and fiery crunch of a big helping of Spiced Date Chili Crisp (page 244), and all will soon be right with the world. Two further pieces of advice: If you can find lamb bacon, try it here! And make the chili crisp well ahead of time, both so that its flavors have time to fully develop and so that you don't have to be fiddling around with it first thing in the morning.

8 thick-cut bacon slices

2 Tbsp butter, at room temperature

8 thick white sandwich bread slices

About ¼ cup [45 g] Spiced Date Chili Crisp (page 244)

Fry up the bacon to your preferred ratio of crispy to floppy, then set it aside on paper towels. Evenly butter one side of each slice of bread, wall to wall. Now is not a time for scrimping. Follow with a goodly quantity of chili crisp, once again evenly spread, and 2 slices of bacon, cut to fit, per sandwich. All will be well.

TREASURES from the GARDEN

THE FOUNTAIN

RAINBOW BOUGAINVILLEA

DAPPLED SUNLIGHT

HOOPOE FEATHER

PALM SHADOWS
ON THE GRASS

HABABUK—
STAGE DATES
in the GARDEN—
the SPRINKLERS
KICKED ON WHILE I WAS PAINTING &
DRENCHED BOTH ME + SKETCHBOOK?

"QUINTESSENTIAL" KHALAS
DATES RIPENING on the
VINE

MY PARENTS' GARDEN IS A TINY PARADISE, A
LEAFY OASIS in the HEART of DUBAI FILLED with
LOVINGLY NURTURED PLANTS. THE DATE PALMS
WERE PLANTED IN WAVES BEGINNING IN 1999, WHEN
WE FIRST MOVED IN. FOR A LONG TIME THEY
WERE TINY: SHORT SQUAT LITTLE TREES LADEN WITH
COMICALLY LARGE BUNCHES of DATES. KHATIB-
SHAPED PALMS. LIKE ALL DATE PALMS, it TOOK THE
TREES SEVERAL YEARS to FULLY MATURE; THEN,
SUDDENLY, THEY SHOT UP, TAPPED INTO the GROUND-
WATER, FOUND THEIR WINGS. NOW THEY ARE ALMOST
NORMAL HEIGHT. IN ANY CASE, THE DATE PALMS
HAVE FRUITED & SURVIVED WHERE OTHER
EXPERIMENTS HAVE NOT: the MANGO TREE, the
MULBERRY, the OLIVE & the POMEGRANATE, the
PERSIAN LIME, the GRAPES on the VINE. NONE
MADE IT, NOT LIKE the DATES.
        COME AUTUMN, MY PARENTS HARVEST
KILOS of DATES FROM EACH of THEIR TREES:
LITTLE LULU DATES, A FAVORITE of MANY IN
the UNITED ARAB EMIRATES, WHICH CAN BE
EATEN at the CRUNCHY KHALAL STAGE AS
WELL AS WHEN FULLY RIPE. BARHI,
HALAWY, KHALAS. THEY DRY THEIR DATE
HARVEST in the SUN, SPREAD ACROSS HUGE
METAL PLATTERS, SHIELDED from VISITING BIRDS
and the LEGIONS of GARDEN CATS BY STRIPY
PLASTIC TABLECLOTHS. THEY EAT the DATES PLAIN,
PRESSED INTO BRICKS, OR ROLLED INTO BALLS COATED
WITH COCONUT & SESAME SEEDS.

from "HAMZA" a POEM.

MY
SISTER,
OUR LAND
HAS A THROBBING
HEART, IT DOESN'T
CEASE to BEAT, AND IT ENDURES
the UNENDURABLE. IT KEEPS
the SECRETS of HILLS and WOMBS. This
LAND SPROUTING WITH SPIKES
and PALMS is also the LAND
THAT GIVES BIRTH to a
FREEDOM FIGHTER.
THIS LAND, MY SISTER, is a
WOMAN.

BY
FADWA TUQAN

drumroll
of COLONIAL FISH

Boiled gray mullet steeped for twenty-four hours in a sauce of milk, rosolio liqueur, capers, and red pepper. To serve, cut it open and fill with date preserves criss-crossed with discs of banana and slices of pineapple. Eat accompanied by a continuous drumroll.

A RECIPE

from the FUTURIST COOK BOOK

formula by the Futurist aeropoet MARINETTI

MAINS

CHAPTER 3

WHOLE ROASTED CAULIFLOWER WITH BRINY OLIVE OIL– CURED CHILES

DINNER FOR 4

This is a big celebratory state of affairs, a textural symphony, producing a cauliflower that is somehow simultaneously yielding and crisp-tender. You can make this recipe with any type of cauliflower, but denser grocery store heads will take longer to cook to tender all the way through. If you can find lacy Chinese cauliflower, it makes for a stunning centerpiece and will develop particularly good crispy bits that trap all the sauce. Romanesco cauliflower, in all of its chartreuse fractal glory, is another strong contender here. The beauty of this recipe, though, is that it will transform the most staid, sensible head of cauliflower into a showstopper of a meal—one that also happens to be vegan.

Don't sleep on the Briny Olive Oil– Cured Chiles (recipe follows): They're the best part. If you don't have time to make them or don't like spicy food, see if you can find fresh pomegranate seeds for the topping, or some other beautiful jewels. This is a big beige dish that needs a little confetti.

If you want a weeknight-friendly version, break up the head of cauliflower and toss the florets in the drizzle, then roast at high heat until translucent and yielding with charred crispy bits.

However you make it, be sure to serve it up like shawarma, with pitas, pickles, salad vegetables, and lots and lots of

Tahini Sauce (recipe follows). You want a nice contrast of crunchy, sour, and fresh to counter the luscious cauliflower and rich tahini-date drizzle.

TAHINI-DATE DRIZZLE

3 Tbsp olive oil

3 Tbsp well-stirred tahini

2 Tbsp date molasses

1 Tbsp apple cider vinegar

1 tsp sweet smoked paprika

1 tsp dried oregano, crumbled between your fingers

½ tsp red pepper flakes

ROASTED CAULIFLOWER

1 head cauliflower

6 dates, pitted and torn into large pieces

6 garlic cloves, smashed with the flat of a knife and peeled

Olive oil, for drizzling

TO SERVE

Briny Olive Oil–Cured Chiles (recipe follows)

Tahini Sauce (recipe follows)

Take your pick, any and all: Pitas, pickles, shaved raw cabbage massaged with a little salt, sliced tomatoes, fresh mint, cilantro, parsley, thinly sliced raw white onion, fresh cucumber sprinkled with lemon juice . . .

CONT'D

TO MAKE THE TAHINI-DATE DRIZZLE, in a medium bowl, stir together the olive oil, tahini, date molasses, vinegar, paprika, oregano, pepper flakes, and 3 tablespoons of water until thoroughly blended. Set aside.

TO MAKE THE ROASTED CAULI-FLOWER, preheat the oven to 400°F [200°C]. Cut off the bottom of the cauliflower so it sits flat. Leave any leaves attached unless they're wilty or otherwise in bad shape. Using the tip of your knife, deeply pierce the bottom of the cauliflower's stem several times, being careful not to sever any florets (this helps the cauliflower cook all the way through). If it's a particularly dense specimen, carefully cut out as much of the core as you can, making sure you aren't structurally compromising your big beautiful cauliflower.

Put the cauliflower in a cast-iron skillet or other ovenproof pan that can hold a full cup of water in its base. Stud the cauliflower with the date pieces and garlic. If you have a loose cauliflower, you can just slide the pieces between the florets and stems; if your cauliflower is more tightly furled, you may need to make incisions with your knife, then stuff the dates and garlic inside. Brush the cauliflower with a thick layer of the tahini-date drizzle, then brush or spoon over a generous amount of olive oil. Pour 1 cup [240 ml] of water into the base of your skillet or pan, loosely cover with aluminum foil, and roast for 30 minutes.

Remove the foil and lower the oven temperature to 350°F [180°C]. Drizzle the cauliflower with more olive oil and roast with the foil off for 15 minutes more. At this point, you are going to start basting the cauliflower with the liquid in the bottom of the skillet and returning it to the oven for several more 15-minute increments. It usually takes me two to three more of these basting/baking cycles to achieve tenderness, but every cauliflower is different. Check, baste, repeat. You'll know it's done when the thickest part of the cauliflower is easily pierced with a knife and the exterior florets are a deep burnished brown, charred in a few places.

Drizzle the cauliflower all over with the tahini sauce, then shower with the olive oil–cured chiles. Serve whole and carve tableside, accompanied by ululations and fanfare. Try to make sure everyone gets a slice with some date and garlic in it—both should be soft and yielding, a built-in sauce. Each diner should assemble their own sandwich by spooning some of the tahini sauce into a pita, then loading up with a few hunks of cauliflower and whatever toppings look good. Feast.

BRINY OLIVE OIL–CURED CHILES

JUST OVER A CUP [240 ML]

8 oz [225 g] fresh chiles (I like long red Dutch peppers, which bring a little heat and a lot of sweetness)

¼ cup [40 g] salt

1 cup [240 ml] olive oil

Cut the chiles into thin rounds. In a medium bowl, toss the chiles with the salt (it looks like a lot of salt, but you really do need it) until completely seasoned, then put the chiles in a fine-mesh sieve or colander set over a bowl and drain for 1 hour. Transfer the chiles to a heatproof medium bowl.

In a small saucepan over medium heat, warm the olive oil to 325°F [165°C], then pour it over the chiles—you should hear them sizzle. Let stand until the chiles come to room temperature. The chiles can be served once they come to room temperature, but they are even better the next day and will keep, covered in oil in an airtight container, in the refrigerator for up to a week. You probably won't use the entire quantity for a single meal, but I wouldn't rule it out if you've got a real chile-head at the table.

TAHINI SAUCE

ABOUT ½ CUP [120G]

¼ cup [60 g] full-fat plain yogurt, labneh, or Greek yogurt

¼ cup [65 g] tahini

Zest of ½ lemon (about 1 tsp)

1 fat garlic clove, grated with a Microplane or very finely minced

Salt

In a small bowl, whisk together the yogurt, tahini, lemon zest, and garlic until smooth. Add water, 1 tablespoon at a time, until the sauce turns pale and is the consistency of pouring cream. Taste and season with salt. This will keep for up to a day in the refrigerator, but it might thicken up; add a little cold water and whisk to thin out again if needed.

BARBECUE MUSHROOM STEAKS WITH CORNBREAD CRUMBLES

DINNER FOR 4, WITH SIDES

This makes a very toothsome main course, dripping with a tangy date molasses–sweetened barbecue sauce and served with lots of complementary sides to amp up the textural contrast. Pressing oyster mushrooms alters their texture, resulting in something that isn't a steak in the traditional sense of the word but that is remarkably satisfying nevertheless: rich, yielding yet snappy, with crispy edges and juicy middles.

Do not commit the two gravest sins against mushrooms, viz

1) Overcrowding the pan.

2) Moving them around before they get a good sear. Leave them be! Your patience will be rewarded.

You can cook maitake, hen-of-the-woods, or other exuberantly fluffy mushrooms this way too. Royal trumpets will also work if you slice them lengthwise into slabs about ½ in [13 mm] thick and cross-hatch their flat surfaces so they can soak up more of the glaze.

2 large clusters oyster mushrooms or 4 smaller clusters, each about the size of your palm

½ cup [120 ml] full-strength Dibs Barbecue Sauce (page 247)

¼ cup [60 ml] beer or water

2 Tbsp neutral, high-heat oil

Salt

Freshly ground black pepper

Cornbread Crumbles (recipe follows)

Labneh "Ranch" (recipe follows)

Assorted raw vegetable crudités, sliced and refreshed in ice water, for serving

Preheat the oven to 400°F [200°C].

If needed, trim the hard stem at the bottom of the mushroom clusters, keeping the clusters as intact as possible—you're aiming for one big piece each.

In a small bowl, whisk together the barbecue sauce and beer or water.

Set a large cast-iron skillet or other ovenproof sauté pan over high heat, getting it as hot as you can (this may take several minutes). Add the oil, followed by the mushrooms, stem-side down. Place another (clean-bottomed!) skillet on top of the mushrooms and weigh it down with cans or other heavy heatproof objects. You should hear sizzling and see liquid start to emerge from the mushrooms. After 2 to 3 minutes, remove the top skillet and generously season the now-pressed mushrooms with salt and pepper. Brush with the barbecue sauce mixture, then flip the mushrooms and repeat the pressing

rigamarole to cook the other side of the mushrooms. Season again with salt and pepper and brush with more barbecue sauce. Continue cooking the mushrooms, flipping them every few minutes, until they begin to char and crisp up on both sides. Spoon a very generous quantity of barbecue sauce over the mushrooms, then slide them into the oven and roast for 10 to 15 minutes, or until the barbecue sauce starts to get a little tacky and caramelize at the edges. Serve sprinkled with a lavish mountain of cornbread crumbles, a side of labneh "ranch," and crunchy vegetables.

CORNBREAD CRUMBLES

2 Tbsp olive oil

2 garlic cloves, grated with a Microplane or very finely minced

1 anchovy (optional)

8¾ oz [250 g] prepared cornbread, torn into pencil eraser–sized crumbs (about 2 cups)

2 Tbsp fresh parsley, minced as finely as possible

While the mushrooms are in the oven, make the crumbles. In a medium skillet over medium-low heat, warm the olive oil. Add the garlic and cook until just golden, 1 to 2 minutes. Add the anchovy (if using) and cook gently until it melts. Tip in the cornbread crumbs and cook, stirring often, until the crumbs turn a deep mahogany color and emit a sweet, toasty fragrance, 3 to 5 minutes. Remove from the heat. Stir in the parsley until you have evenly distributed flecks of green amid the cornbread's deep gold. Set aside.

LABNEH "RANCH"

½ cup [120 g] labneh or very thick Greek yogurt

¼ cup [60 g] mayonnaise, preferably Kewpie-style

3 scallions (white and green parts), finely minced

1 garlic clove, grated with a Microplane or very finely minced

1 Tbsp dried parsley

1 tsp dried dill

1 tsp fish sauce (optional but encouraged)

About ¼ tsp red pepper flakes

Salt

Freshly ground black pepper

In a medium bowl, whisk together the labneh, mayonnaise, scallions, garlic, parsley, dill, fish sauce (if using), and red pepper flakes. Taste and season with salt and pepper. This will keep, in an airtight container in the refrigerator, for up to 3 days. Use to dress salads, as a dip for hard-boiled eggs, as a superior companion for French fries . . . and so on.

BULGUR MUJADARRA

DINNER AND LEFTOVERS FOR 4

Mujadarra is big comfort food in our house—a hearty rustic tangle of caramelized onion, earthy lentils, bright lemon juice, and smoky cumin-scented rice or bulgur. The ingredients are humble, but the end result is complex and deeply soothing. I've added a couple of nontraditional ingredients to reflect the way we like to eat it—with sweet pops of date to complement the onions and a full-fisted quantity of arugula—which also turns it into a complete meal. The quantities given here make a ton, but leftovers reheat well for several days.

Use the lentil water to cook the bulgur; this ensures your cumin works twice as hard and lends the starchy goodness of the lentil-enriched broth to the finished dish. And if you own a pair of swim goggles, consider wearing them while you chop the onions: You will look ridiculous, but at least you won't be weeping.

Serve the finished dish drizzled with generous quantities of olive oil to bring everything together.

¾ cup [180 ml] olive oil for cooking, plus a big glug for drizzling

5 medium onions, halved and cut into ¼ in [6 mm] moons

3 cups [710 ml] broth or water

2 cups [400 g] brown lentils, picked over and rinsed

2 Tbsp ground cumin

About 1 tsp salt

2 cups [300 g] fine bulgur

Juice of 2 lemons

8 large or 12 small dates, pitted and roughly chopped

3 to 4 big handfuls baby arugula or other tender greens

Flaky salt

Freshly ground black pepper

In a large, deep skillet over medium heat, warm ¾ cup [180 ml] of olive oil until hot and shiny. Gently tip in the onions and stir to coat them in the oil. Increase the heat to medium-high and cook, stirring frequently, for about 20 minutes, or until the onions are tender, floppy, and yielding—they should be deeply golden brown but not completely caramelized. Remove from the heat and set aside.

Meanwhile, in a large pot with a tight-fitting lid (you'll need it later), combine the broth or water, lentils, and cumin. Add the salt, but use less if your broth is salty. Bring to a boil, then lower the heat and simmer, adding more water if needed, until the lentils are tender but not mushy, 15 to 30 minutes depending on your lentils. Drain the lentils and return them to the pot, reserving the cumin-scented lentil water. Measure this water. If you don't have 4 cups [945 ml], add broth or water to make up the difference.

Add the bulgur, along with the 4 cups [945 ml] of lentil water, to the lentils in the pot and bring to a boil. Continue boiling for 3 minutes, then remove from the heat, cover, and let stand until the bulgur is completely hydrated and tender and the lentils are soft, 15 to 20 minutes. The liquid should be completely absorbed at this point; if it isn't, turn the heat back on low and stir gently until it is. Taste and season with salt.

In a very large salad bowl, toss the lentils and bulgur with the cooked onions, lemon juice, the big glug of finishing olive oil, the dates, and the arugula. Get everything evenly distributed, then taste and finesse with flaky salt, pepper, and more olive oil if needed. Serve hot or at room temperature. Leftovers will keep, in an airtight container in the refrigerator, for a couple of days, and up to a week if you leave the arugula out and only add before you want to eat.

SKILLET CHICKEN & FREEKEH

DINNER FOR 4

This one-pan chicken dinner features smoky freekeh coated in a bright, briny, chicken fat–infused broth. If you can find Barhi dates, use them here. Their caramel notes play well against the earthy freekeh, and they are also around the size and shape of the Castelvetrano olives—pleasant little orbs. This recipe will, however, work with almost any combination of date, olive, and citrus, so feel free to riff to your heart's content. I leave the pits in both the olives and the dates for a more rustic vibe (and because this is meant to be an easy, one-pan weeknight dinner), but you can absolutely remove the pits before cooking if you wish.

PICKLED RED ONIONS

1 small red onion, cut into thin half-moons

3 Tbsp apple cider vinegar

½ tsp sugar

¼ tsp salt

CHICKEN

4 skin-on, bone-in chicken thighs

Salt

Freshly ground black pepper

1 Tbsp olive oil

8 garlic cloves, smashed with the flat of a knife and peeled

3 shallots, peeled and halved lengthwise

1 cup [150 g] cracked freekeh, picked over for debris and rinsed

½ cup [60 g] olives (about 12 olives)

8 dates

1 lemon, scrubbed, cut crosswise into thick slices, and seeded

Big pinch of red pepper flakes

Flaky salt, for finishing

TO PICKLE THE RED ONIONS, in a small, nonreactive bowl or jar, combine the red onion, vinegar, sugar, salt, and 2 tablespoons of cold water. Set aside until you're done with the chicken. The onions will be ready to eat by the time you've finished cooking, but if you can make these a few hours in advance, they'll be even better.

TO MAKE THE CHICKEN, season the thighs all over with salt and pepper. In a deep cast-iron skillet over medium heat, warm the olive oil. Add the chicken thighs, skin-side down, and sear without moving them around until the chicken skin is a deep golden brown and much of the fat has rendered into the pan, 5 to 8 minutes. Don't be tempted to peek to see how the chicken is doing until at least 5 minutes have gone by.

Transfer the partially cooked chicken to a plate and set aside.

Add the garlic and shallots to the rendered chicken fat in the skillet and cook, stirring, until aromatic and lightly golden, 2 to 3 minutes. Add the freekeh and stir to cover each grain in the fat. Cook, stirring, until the freekeh starts to smell appetizingly toasty, 3 to 4 minutes. Add the olives and dates and stir just to distribute evenly across the pan. Add 2 cups [475 ml] of water and deglaze the pan, scraping up any browned bits from the bottom. Arrange 4 lemon slices on top of the freekeh mixture, then perch the chicken thighs, skin-side up, directly on top of each lemon slice. Pour in any accumulated chicken juices. If you have any extra lemon slices, arrange them in the pan as well. Sprinkle with red pepper flakes. Bring to a boil, then cover, turn the heat to low, and simmer for 20 minutes. At this point, the dates will have plumped, the citrus slices will be yielding and jammy, and the freekeh will be totally cooked through—tender but with a slight bite to it.

Remove the lid and continue to simmer until the remaining liquid in the pan is thickened, glossy, and reduced, about 5 minutes. If you dip

CONT'D

a wooden spoon into the freekeh at this point, the liquid should coat the back of the spoon, and if you run your finger across the back of the spoon, you should see a clear line. If it seems like there is still too much liquid, don't worry—it will thicken up as it sits. Season with salt and pepper—it might take the salt a minute to soak in, so add it in stages, tasting as you go.

Sprinkle with the pickled red onion and flaky salt, and serve straight from the skillet with a side salad of something bracingly acidic and crunchy (try the Shaved Celery Salad with Spiced Date Chili Crisp, page 160).

MALAI CHICKEN WITH CREAMY STUFFED DATES

DINNER FOR 4, WITH FLATBREADS OR RICE

Using cheese to add richness and flavor to a marinade is a classic trick from the British Indian restaurant playbook. If you plan ahead, it's really worth giving the chicken 48 hours to soak up the marinade and tenderize in the yogurt. This recipe was written for a home oven, but it is also a treat when grilled: Thread the chicken and dates onto separate skewers to allow for their different grill times. Serve bundled into warm roti or naan, with a little squeeze of fresh lime, a scattering of cilantro, and a pile of fresh or Pickled Red Onions (page 113). The Briny Olive Oil–Cured Chiles (page 109) make another lovely addition.

2 Tbsp ghee or butter

1 tsp whole cumin seeds

1 tsp ground turmeric

1 tsp red chili powder

½ tsp salt

6 garlic cloves, grated with a Microplane, very finely minced, or smashed to a paste using a mortar and pestle

1 Tbsp fresh ginger, grated with a Microplane or very finely minced

2 tsp malt vinegar or another tart vinegar

½ cup [120 ml] heavy cream

½ cup [120 g] labneh or thick yogurt

3 oz [85 g] mild Cheddar or Amul cheese, finely grated

¼ cup [12 g] finely chopped cilantro leaves and stems

1 Tbsp date sugar or ½ Tbsp packed light brown sugar

4 boneless, skinless chicken thighs (about 2 lbs [910 g]), cut into bite-size pieces

12 big juicy dates, such as Medjools

To bloom the spices, in a small saucepan over medium-low heat, melt the ghee and stir in the cumin, turmeric, chili powder, and salt. Cook until the spices are spluttering and fragrant but not burnt. Remove from the heat, then stir in the garlic, ginger, and vinegar. Let cool to lukewarm while you prep the rest of the marinade.

In a large bowl, stir together the heavy cream, labneh, grated cheese, cilantro, and date sugar until completely smooth. Mix in the cooled spiced ghee. The marinade will turn a lovely sunny yellow and look thick and fluffy.

Tumble in the chicken pieces and coat thoroughly. Cover and refrigerate for at least 1 hour and up to 48 hours—the longer you marinate the chicken, the more tender and flavorful the result.

Preheat the oven to 400°F [200°C]. Line one or two baking sheets with parchment paper. Spread the chicken pieces out in a single layer on the prepared baking sheet or sheets, reserving the marinade. Distribute the chicken across two baking sheets if need be, so that the hot oven air can circulate around all the bits and pieces.

Pit the dates but don't fully halve them. Stuff each date with a generous spoonful of the leftover marinade and press to close them, then coat the outsides in the marinade too. Spread the dates out on the baking sheet(s), dotted among the chicken. Bake for 20 to 25 minutes, or until the chicken is golden and caramelized and the dates are gooey and their stuffing is fully cooked. If need be, broil for the last couple of minutes to get a hint of char. Serve hot. Leftovers will keep, refrigerated in an airtight container, for up to 3 days.

STICKY GLAZED POUSSINS WITH TOASTED NUTS & SEEDS

DINNER FOR 4 TO 6, DEPENDING ON SIDES

A festive centerpiece, these tender little date-glazed chickens glisten underneath a dramatic mountain of toasty, seedy rubble. Growing up, we often marked special occasions with a Shami-style roast chicken perched on a bed of hashweh-spiced, rice studded with ground beef and festooned with fried pine nuts and almonds. This adaptation takes the garnish to a whole new level of crunch.

The ingredient list may seem long, with lots of fiddly bits, but if you can't find an ingredient, feel free to substitute something similar or simply skip it. If you don't have both white and black pepper, for instance, just use what you have. Despite the many ingredients, the recipe is simple to make and results in a tender, fully flavored chicken with crunchy little flavor explosions from the nuts and seeds, all nestled in a bed of fragrant spiced rice. *Hashweh* means "stuffing" in many Shami (Levantine) dialects—you can stuff the birds with the rice too—but it's often served as an accompaniment to meat and poultry dishes. Start the recipe a day in advance, if you can, to give the spice mix time to do its work. Finally, if you can't find poussins or Cornish game hens, use one large roasting chicken and increase the initial oven time to 40 minutes before you start basting with the date molasses mixture.

HASHWEH SPICE MIX

1½ Tbsp salt

1½ Tbsp ground allspice

1½ Tbsp ground cinnamon

2 tsp ground cardamom

2 tsp ground ginger

2 tsp freshly ground black pepper

1 tsp ground white pepper

1 tsp ground cloves

1 tsp freshly grated nutmeg

1 tsp sugar

POUSSINS

2 poussins or Cornish game hens, patted dry

2 Tbsp olive oil

DATE BASTING LIQUID

¼ cup [60 ml] date molasses

¼ cup [60 ml] olive oil

SPICED RICE

2 cups [400 g] basmati rice

1 Tbsp olive oil

10 oz [285 g] ground beef

2 cups [475 ml] boiling water

SEEDY RUBBLE

3 Tbsp olive oil

½ cup [60 g] lightly crushed pistachios

½ cup [60 g] lightly crushed pine nuts

2 Tbsp mild red chili flakes, such as Aleppo or Urfa biber (or less if you want less spice)

2 Tbsp sesame seeds (black, white, or both)

2 Tbsp chia seeds

2 tsp yellow mustard seeds

2 Tbsp store-bought crispy fried shallots

Salt

Small handful fresh mint and/or parsley, for finishing

TO MAKE THE HASHWEH SPICE MIX, in a small bowl, stir together the salt, allspice, cinnamon, cardamom, ginger, black pepper, white pepper, cloves, nutmeg, and sugar. Divide the mixture into two equal portions; you will use half as a dry brine for your poussins and half to flavor the rice.

TO PREPARE THE POUSSINS, use a hooked index finger to gently separate the skin from the flesh of the birds over the breastbone and around the legs and thighs. It should come apart quite easily, but go slowly and try not to tear holes in the skin.

CONT'D

Rub the dry brine portion of the spice blend all over the poussins, inside and out, as well as underneath the skin. Really get in there. Refrigerate and air-chill the birds, uncovered, for at least 4 hours and up to overnight. Resting the uncovered birds in the dry, cold refrigerator air helps to dry out the skin and will result in a crispier bird.

TO MAKE THE DATE BASTING LIQUID, in a small bowl, combine the date molasses with 2 tablespoons of hot water. Add the olive oil and stir to thoroughly combine. Set aside.

Set an oven rack in the bottom third of the oven and preheat the oven to 350°F [180°C]. Arrange a roasting rack in a roasting pan or on a rimmed baking sheet. If you don't have a roasting rack, you can put the birds directly on the pan, but it's better to have hot air circulating all around them if possible.

Put the birds, breast-side up, on the roasting rack and rub 1 tablespoon of olive oil all over each one. Roast for 30 minutes, then raise the oven temperature to 400°F [200°C]. Use a pastry brush or basting brush to coat the birds with the date basting liquid and return to the oven for 5 minutes. Pull the birds out of the oven again and brush them all over with the date basting liquid again.

Repeat this process at least two more times, checking on the birds every 5 minutes and building up layers of molasses until the skin is glossy and bronzed, with darker patches. Keep any unused date basting liquid for the final plating. The poussins are done if the juices run clear when the thickest part of the thigh is pierced with a knife. Let the birds rest for at least 10 minutes and up to 30 minutes.

While the birds roast, **MAKE THE RICE:** In a large bowl, combine the rice with enough cold water to cover it by a few inches. Stir the rice with your fingers to release the starches, then let the rice settle. Pour off the water. Repeat this process twice, then let the drained rice sit for 10 minutes or so while you cook the beef.

In a large pot with a tight-fitting lid over medium-high heat, warm the olive oil. Add the ground beef and brown it, using a wooden spoon to break apart any large clumps, for about 3 minutes. Add the remaining portion of the hashweh spice mix and stir to evenly distribute it throughout the beef. Continue cooking, stirring occasionally, for another 1 to 2 minutes, or until the meat is thoroughly golden. Turn the heat to low and cook for another 4 minutes. Turn the heat back up to high, then

tip the drained rice into the pot. Cook, stirring vigorously, for another 3 to 4 minutes, or until the rice starts to smell toasted and is slightly translucent at the edges. Add the boiling water and stir to scrape up any browned spices and meaty bits at the bottom of the pot. Dial down the heat to as low as possible, cover, then cook, undisturbed, for 20 minutes. Don't take the lid off; just leave it alone. After 20 minutes, remove from the heat but leave the lid on and let the rice rest and fully open up for at least another 10 minutes and up to 30 minutes.

TO MAKE THE SEEDY RUBBLE, in a medium skillet over medium heat, warm the olive oil. Add the pistachios and pine nuts and toast, stirring frequently, until fragrant and just starting to turn faintly golden, 2 to 3 minutes. Add the chili flakes, sesame seeds, chia seeds, and mustard seeds and toast for another minute. Remove from the heat, then add the crispy fried shallots and season with salt. The rubble is ready to eat as soon as it's cool, but it definitely benefits from sitting for even 15 minutes for the flavors to meld—the only danger is that you may eat it all before it makes it to the final dish. If you are lucky enough to have any left over, it is good on pretty much anything and

will keep in an airtight container at room temperature for up to 4 days.

TO PLATE, spoon about two-thirds of the rice onto a platter and gently place the poussins on top, then mound the rest of the rice around them. Brush each poussin with the last of the date basting liquid to make them sticky, then pile the seedy rubble on top. Really make a mountain of it; you want the rubble to tumble into the rice and mingle with the grains when you spoon it up. Sprinkle with torn fresh mint and/ or parsley and serve to your lucky fellow diners. Leftovers will keep, in an airtight container in the refrigerator, for up to 3 days.

DRY-BRINED ROAST DUCK WITH CUMIN & FENNEL SEEDS

DINNER FOR 4

This makes a crackly-skinned roast duck, popping with little bursts of flavor from the cumin and fennel seeds, and enlisting the aid of date sugar to draw out the complex sweetness of the meat. Roast duck is the default celebration dish in our house, and I have spent many years perfecting this technique for the crispiest skin and juiciest meat with a minimum of fuss, walking it back from a three-day extravaganza involving obsessive pin-pricking of the skin, kettles of boiling water, and mail-ordered maltose for lacquering purposes. This relatively streamlined approach combines the power of a dry rub with the air-chilling capabilities of your home refrigerator. Leaving the duck in there overnight, uncovered, ensures the skin gets totally dry and crisps up fully in the heat of the oven. And separating the skin from the flesh, then applying the dry rub, means the rub penetrates and seasons the flesh directly, instead of just sitting on top of the skin. While the duck is roasting, the fat from the skin is also able to drip onto the meat, effectively basting it and keeping it moist.

Start this recipe the night before you plan to eat to allow for ample air-chilling time.

One 4 to 5 lb duck (Long Island or Peking duck is preferable, but any kind you can get will do)

1 recipe Umm Qais's Grilling Spices (page 246)

Examine your duck. If there is a little baggie of giblets and liver in its cavity, pull it out and use its contents to make yourself a chef's snack: Sauté in butter and pomegranate molasses, then drape over hot slices of toast, and eat. Now you are fortified for the task ahead. If there are any large quills or feathers left in the duck's skin, use tweezers to pull them out. The first time I roasted a duck, I was surprised to find a bunch of spiky quills left in, and you may be too. You don't have to pull them out—they will crisp up in the oven—but it can be an oddly satisfying activity, like popping bubble wrap.

Next, separate the duck's skin from its flesh, keeping the skin in one piece. You can do this using your hands, a chopstick, a knife—whatever gets the job done. Don't be squeamish and really get in there, but keep your pressure even and try not to tear the skin. (If it does tear, don't worry—the duck will still be delicious, it just might not look quite as pretty.) It's most important to separate the skin over the breast meat and thighs. You

can do this by hooking your finger and pulling smoothly and firmly to release the skin. I find a knife can sometimes be helpful to get things going, particularly at the seam down the center of the breast.

Prick the duck's skin all over using a toothpick, knife tip, or sturdy needle. Be careful to only pierce the skin and not the flesh below.

Rub the grilling spices under and over the duck's skin and inside its cavity.

Place the duck on a roasting rack or cooling rack set inside a pan (for air circulation purposes) and air chill in the refrigerator, uncovered, for at least 8 hours and up to 48 hours. Keeping it uncovered helps to draw out moisture and is what will get you that super crispy duck skin later. The next day, the color and texture of the duck skin should be visibly different: tighter, darker, and less flabby.

Preheat the oven to 300°F [150°C]. Set a rack in a very stable and deep-sided roasting pan.

Place the duck, breast-side up, on the rack, then pour about 1 cup [240 ml] of water into the roasting pan. This keeps the dripping duck fat from smoking out your oven. Don't overfill the pan, because then you run the risk of the greasy water slopping out and setting off your fire alarm and annoying all the neighbors (ask me how I know). Unlike other poultry, you want to start duck in the oven while it's still chilled—the low oven temperature and cool skin give the duck fat time to render out gently and evenly. Roast for 1 hour, then flip the duck so it is breast-side down and roast for another hour. Flip the duck again so it is breast-side up and roast for another 30 minutes—about 2½ hours in total. Crank the heat up to 375°F [190°C] for the final 15 minutes, but keep an eye on things as the date sugar in the rub can burn very quickly. The duck's internal temperature should measure at about 140°F [60°C] when pierced in the thickest part of the breast. Let it rest for 10 to 15 minutes before you serve it forth as the centerpiece of your feast. Leftover duck will keep, refrigerated in an airtight container, for up to 4 days.

BEEF & PISTACHIO MEATBALLS

MEATBALLS FOR 4

These tiny-but-mighty bites sit somewhere between a kebab and a meatball. With a tender, loose texture, the pistachios and dates are held together by a lattice of juicy meat. Made right, each meatball should fall apart when popped whole into your mouth, letting all of the elements—the sweet dates, rich pistachios, bright herbs, and smoky, earthy spices—mingle in one rush of flavor. Be as delicate as possible when blending the meatball mixture. The lighter your touch, the more tender the result. The grated onion is the secret ingredient binding everything together. Unlike milk, eggs, or breadcrumbs, it won't mask the other flavors but will elevate them.

If all you can find is lean beef, mix in a tablespoon of ghee to add oomph—or better yet, use ground lamb instead.

½ onion, grated using the coarse holes of a box grater

¼ cup [10 g] lightly packed chopped fresh mint, plus more for serving

¼ cup [10 g] lightly packed chopped fresh flat-leaf parsley

¼ cup [30 g] roughly chopped raw or roasted unsalted pistachios

6 dates, pitted and roughly chopped

¼ cup [20 g] finely chopped jalapeño (about 1 medium pepper)

1 Tbsp olive oil, plus more if needed

1 tsp ground cumin

1 tsp sweet smoked paprika

1 tsp salt, plus finishing salt at the end

Several generous grinds freshly ground black pepper

1 lb [450 g] fatty ground beef

Labneh or very thick Greek yogurt, for plating

Preheat the oven to 450°F [230°C].

In a large bowl, combine the onion, mint, parsley, pistachios, dates, jalapeño, olive oil, cumin, paprika, salt, and pepper. Mix together with your hands until evenly blended. Add the ground beef and gently work the ingredients together, using your fingers to push and fold everything together. Try not to overmix, or you will end up with rubbery, tough meatballs. Test the seasoning by frying a small spoonful of the mixture in a skillet or sauté pan, or microwaving it for 30 seconds, until just cooked. Taste and adjust the seasoning, particularly the salt, if necessary.

Using a half-tablespoon measure, portion out dollops of the meat mixture onto a rimmed baking sheet, leaving about 1 in [2.5 cm] between the meatballs—they emit juices as they cook.

Add about 1 teaspoon of olive oil to a bowl of water that is large enough to dip your hand into. Flick your fingers through the water to separate the oil into droplets, then use your wet hands to gently shape the meatballs into pleasant orbs, dipping your fingers back into the oil/water mixture as necessary to prevent the meat from sticking to you.

Bake the meatballs until they are lightly browned and no longer pink in the center, 7 to 9 minutes. Serve hot, tumbled onto a schmear of labneh or yogurt and sprinkled with more chopped fresh mint and salt. Leftover meatballs will keep, refrigerated in an airtight container, for up to 3 days.

RIB EYE STEAK WITH A SALT & DATE SUGAR CRUST

STEAK FOR 2, WITH SIDES

Here are two perhaps counterintuitive things you can do to a big honking piece of meat: coat it in sugar and baste it with butter. Date sugar acts as a tenderizer; when combined in a rub with salt, it helps to gently season the meat all the way through without making it overly sweet. And butter basting is a luxe-feeling yet simple way to treat a $$$ cut of meat.

Start this recipe a full day ahead to give the rub time to work its magic. Serve it with something light and bright and sparkling alongside to counteract the richness of the meat: a crunchy salad of apples and endive tossed with a sharp mustardy dressing, perhaps, or thinly sliced celery and clementine segments with a dressing of red wine vinegar, clementine juice, olive oil, and a dash each of sesame oil and soy sauce.

This recipe serves two; if you want to make more steaks, the rub scales up well, but keep in mind that you will only be able to fit one steak in a skillet at a time.

3 Tbsp date sugar

1½ Tbsp flaky salt, such as Maldon

1 bone-in rib eye steak, at least 1 in [2.5 cm] thick

1 Tbsp ghee or high-heat cooking oil

3 Tbsp butter

3 garlic cloves, smashed with the flat of a knife and peeled

2 mint sprigs

2 oregano sprigs

In a small bowl, combine the date sugar and salt. Use about half of this mixture to generously coat the steak on both sides and along its fatty seam. Loosely cover the steak and rest it in the refrigerator for at least 2 hours and preferably 24 hours. The longer rest really makes a difference! About 30 minutes before you're ready to eat, remove the steak from the refrigerator and let it come to room temperature.

Preheat the oven to 400°F [200°C]. Use the remaining date sugar and salt mixture to reseason the steak just before you cook it.

Place an ovenproof cast-iron skillet or heavy sauté pan over medium-high heat. You don't want it ripping hot, because the date sugar will burn right away instead of caramelizing (a little charring is fine). Add the ghee or oil, followed by the steak. Sear the steak for 3 to 4 minutes on each side, then stand it on the fatty edge for 2 minutes to get some color there as well.

Slide the steak, still in the skillet, into the oven for 8 minutes, or until it registers 130°F [55°C] on an instant-read thermometer.

Pull the skillet out of the oven and return it to the stovetop. Drop in the butter, smashed garlic, mint, and oregano. The butter should start to melt on contact with the hot metal, but turn the heat to low if needed to help with this process. Carefully tilt the pan, so the garlic and herbs are at the bottom of the pan and the steak is at the top. Use a large spoon to gather the butter that runs down to the bottom of the pan and baste the steak continuously for 2 minutes or so—the fragrant butter will run off the steak and back into the garlicky-herby pool for you to spoon up again. Flip the steak and baste for another 2 minutes on the other side. This is a very satisfying activity.

Transfer the steak to a cutting board and let it rest, uncovered, for 10 minutes. Cut the steak off the bone, then cut it into slices. Serve with the pan juices alongside.

BEEF SHANK RUTABIYYA WITH PRESERVED LEMON GREMOLATA

DINNER FOR 6 TO 8, WITH BREAD FOR MOP-UP DUTY

The "rutab" in the title of this tagine-like dish refers to fresh dates at the rutab stage, when they are soft and custardy and before they have been sun-dried. This recipe was inspired by a category of medieval Islamic trickster stews, where stuffed kebabs were playfully disguised as all manner of other foods to bring delight to guests. In *Kitab al-Tabikh*, the seminal cookbook by al-Baghdadi dating to 1226 CE, a recipe for a dish also called Rutabi-yya encouraged cooks to cook "long meatballs colored with saffron and shaped like dates" and serve them in a stew strewn with real dates, all to surprise unsuspecting diners. You can try this method, or just use beef shanks instead. Look for thick osso buco–style cross-cut shanks, but if you can't find beef shanks, try short ribs or oxtail.

When rutab dates are in season in early fall, you can often find them fresh in the produce aisle of Middle Eastern grocery stores. Otherwise, you can sometimes find them in the freezer aisle. You can also make this dish with regular dates at any time of year; just add them to the pot for an extra 5 to 10 minutes, so they slump and suc-cumb to the sauce.

Finally, it is really worth seeking out preserved lemons to make the gremolata, but if you can't find them,

use a combination of salt and fresh lemon zest and juice. The salty, briny, vegetal brightness of the gremolata is a necessary counterpoint to the sweet, tender meat.

3 lbs [1.4 kg] osso buco–style cross-cut beef shanks, 2½ to 3 in [6 to 7½ cm] thick

About ¼ cup [35 g] flour

¼ cup [60 ml] olive oil

2 large onions, finely chopped

Big pinch of saffron (about 15 threads)

2 tsp ground ginger

2 tsp ground cinnamon

Salt

Freshly ground black pepper

2 to 3 cups [475 to 700 ml] beef or chicken broth

PRESERVED LEMON GREMOLATA

1 bunch fresh flat-leaf parsley, minced

1 preserved lemon, innards and pith discarded and peel finely minced

2 garlic cloves, finely minced

4 to 8 oz [115 to 225 g] rutab dates, pitted

⅓ cup [40 g] toasted slivered almonds

2 Tbsp toasted white sesame seeds

Warm fresh bread, for serving

Preheat the oven to 350°F [180°C].

Remove the beef shanks from the refrigerator 30 minutes before you want to start cooking and let them come to room temperature. If using an osso buco–style cut, check to see that the membrane of trans-parent skin wrapping the meat is still there; if it isn't, tie each shank with string to hold the meat around the bone during the long cooking time. Coat the beef shanks in a light dust-ing of flour and tap off any excess.

In a Dutch oven large enough to hold all the meat in a single layer or another ovenproof vessel with a tight-fitting lid, heat the olive oil over medium-high heat. Working in batches if needed, sear the shanks until golden brown, 3 to 4 minutes per side. Remove the shanks from the pot and set aside. Tip in the onions, saffron, ginger, and cinna-mon and stir to coat in the fat left in the pot. Season with salt and pepper. Add 2 cups [475 ml] of the beef or chicken broth and deglaze the pan, scraping up any browned bits from the bottom. Nestle the shanks in the onion mixture, then top up with additional broth if needed—the liquid should come about three-quarters of the way up the meat, not fully submerge it. Cover the pot, slide it

CONT'D

into the oven, and braise, basting the meat about every 30 minutes, until tender, at least 1½ hours and up to 3½ hours. The meat is done when it breaks apart with the gentle pressure of a spoon.

Meanwhile, **TO MAKE THE GREMOLATA**, in a medium bowl, mix together the parsley, preserved lemon, and garlic. Set aside until ready to serve.

When the meat is ready, add the dates to the pot and return to the oven for an additional 10 minutes, or until the dates are tender and yielding and have absorbed some of the flavors of the sauce. Remove the stew from the oven and let stand, covered, for 10 to 15 minutes so the flavors can settle. Taste and season with salt and pepper if needed, keeping in mind that the gremolata is already quite salty.

Serve the stew sprinkled with the almonds and sesame seeds and accompanied by lots of warm fresh bread and the gremolata. Be sure to scoop out and eat the marrow—it's the official "best bit" and the part we used to fight over as kids. As with any stew, this will taste better the day after you make it (and it keeps, in an airtight container in the refrigerator, for up to 5 days), but the gremolata is best eaten the day you prepare it.

MACAROUNA BIL LABAN

DINNER FOR 4

Pure comfort food. Think of this dish as yogurt-inflected Middle Eastern mac 'n' cheese, a speedy weeknight meal whipped together by tired parents throughout the region. The spiced ground beef is ready in the time it takes to boil the water for the pasta, and by the time the pasta is done, you've stirred together the no-cook garlicky yogurt sauce. It's beloved by children of all ages, as well as zonked adults who want a warm bowl of something soothing but not boring at the end of a long day. The dates are an unconventional but really very compelling addition (I promise!).

1 lb [450 g] dried pasta, cozy shape of your choice (I like elbows)

6 Tbsp [90 ml] olive oil, plus more for serving

1 red onion, diced

1 lb [450 g] ground beef

1 tsp salt

1 tsp ground cinnamon

1 tsp ground allspice

⅓ cup [40 g] slivered almonds or pine nuts or pistachios

5 dates, pitted and chopped into pieces about the size of a pencil eraser

⅓ cup [20 g] chopped fresh flat-leaf parsley

Freshly ground black pepper

YOGURT SAUCE

1 lb [450 g] labneh or thick Greek yogurt

3 garlic cloves, finely minced or grated with a Microplane

Juice of 1 lemon, plus more for serving

½ tsp salt

Bring a large pot of salted water to a boil over high heat. Add the pasta and cook until al dente, 1 to 2 minutes less than the cooking time on the box. Reserve about 1 cup [240 ml] of the pasta cooking water, then drain the pasta.

Meanwhile, in a large skillet or sauté pan over medium heat, warm 3 tablespoons of the olive oil. Add the onion and cook, stirring occasionally, until softened and translucent but not browned, about 5 minutes. Add the ground beef, salt, cinnamon, and allspice and cook, using a wooden spoon to break apart any large clumps of meat, until the beef is completely cooked through, golden brown, and slightly crispy, about 8 minutes. Transfer the beef, onion, and any drippings to a bowl and set aside. Add the remaining 3 tablespoons of olive oil to the skillet, then add the almonds and toast, stirring continuously, until deeply golden, about 4 minutes. Add the almonds to the beef, followed by the dates and parsley. Mix well, taste, and season with salt and pepper if needed.

TO MAKE THE YOGURT SAUCE, in a medium bowl, mix together the yogurt, garlic, lemon juice, and salt. Add just enough pasta water to give it the consistency of thick pouring cream.

Add the yogurt sauce to the drained pasta and toss to coat; the sauce should be thick enough to coat the pasta like mac 'n' cheese. Serve the pasta in bowls with the beef and onions mounded on top, along with a fresh drizzle of olive oil and a squeeze of lemon juice. Season with salt and pepper.

Leftovers will keep, refrigerated, for up to 3 days.

MILK-BRAISED LAMB SHANKS WITH MUGHAL SPICES

DINNER FOR 6, WITH SIDES

This braising method enlists the power of milk proteins to tenderize the meat, resulting in a beautifully textured, full-flavored dish fit for a Mughal emperor. Although this milk-braising technique is not one that would have been used in a royal court, any member of the Mughal dynasty would have appreciated a meal that combines aromatic warm spices, dried fruit, and dairy.

As it cooks down, the milk caramelizes to form a lush, lamby, velvety cloak that you purée with dates and spices to create an extremely rich sauce. While braising is a long process, most of it is hands-off—and your home will smell increasingly amazing as the hours tick by. Served with saffron rice and a bright crunchy salad of something like pomegranate and shaved fennel, this makes a perfect meal for a cold wintry day.

**3 large lamb shanks,
about 1 lb [455 g] each**

Salt and black pepper

1 Tbsp neutral oil or ghee

**2 cups [475 ml] whole milk,
plus more if needed**

1 cinnamon stick

1 tsp whole fennel seeds

1 tsp ground ginger

1 tsp ground turmeric

1 tsp red pepper flakes

6 dates, pitted

Up to 2 Tbsp rosewater

Fresh or dried organic rose or marigold petals and crushed raw pistachios, for garnishing

Generously season the lamb shanks with salt and let stand for 1 hour at room temperature or up to overnight in the refrigerator.

In a heavy-bottom pot with a tight-fitting lid or a Dutch oven large enough to fit all the meat in a single layer, heat the oil or ghee over medium-high heat. Working in batches if needed, brown the shanks on all sides, about 8 minutes total per batch. You will develop much of the flavor during this sear, so don't be shy and really let the lamb brown. Pour in the milk and deglaze the pan, scraping up any browned bits from the bottom. The liquid should come about two-thirds of the way up the shanks; if not, add more milk or water. Add the cinnamon stick, fennel seeds, ginger, turmeric, and red pepper flakes and stir to incorporate. Bring to a simmer, then turn the heat to low, cover with a tight-fitting lid, and braise for 2 to 3 hours. Check on the meat every so often, turning the shanks over and giving the sauce

a gentle stir to make sure it is not catching on the bottom of the pan and burning. The meat is done when it is tender and giving and about to fall off the bone. At this point, the braising liquid will smell beautiful, but it will appear to have curdled into large, ricotta-like blobs and the milk fat will have separated into golden puddles. Don't worry—you will purée the sauce later.

Remove the shanks from the pot and set aside in a warmish place. Fish out and discard the cinnamon stick. Add the dates to the sauce. Using an immersion blender, blitz the sauce in the pot until it is velvety and smooth and the dates are fully incorporated. If you don't have an immersion blender, you can use a regular blender and purée in batches. Be careful, as it is hot. (If you're feeling lazy, you don't need to blend the sauce at all, but it will benefit from a good whisking to emulsify the fats and the solids and make it look more visually appealing and less lumpy.)

Taste the sauce and add salt and black pepper if needed. Stir in 1 tablespoon of the rosewater, then taste the sauce and add additional rosewater only if you feel it's necessary. You're looking for a mere floral whisper in the background, almost impossible to place but adding a certain magical element to the entire proceedings. It's much easier to increase the amount of rosewater than to muffle it once it's having its way with your sauce, so be gentle and taste as you go.

Arrange the shanks on a rimmed serving platter and pour the sauce over them. Finish with rose or marigold petals, crushed between your fingertips, and a scatter of bright green pistachios. Leftovers will keep, tightly covered in the refrigerator, for up to 3 days.

SPICY CUMIN LAMB CHOPS

DINNER 4, WITH SIDES

This recipe was inspired by the combination of lamb and cumin that is so prevalent in Muslim Chinese food. Here, the smoky cumin and musky lamb pair beautifully with a tangle of oven-sweetened onions and dates. You'll need an ovenproof skillet for this recipe, but if you don't have one, you can roast the onions and dates on a rimmed baking sheet, tented with foil, and then place the lamb chops directly on the baking sheet and slide it back into the oven.

Four lamb shoulder chops, 5 to 7 oz [150 to 200 g] each

Salt

1 red onion, cut into ½ in [13 mm] thick half-moons

2 Tbsp olive oil

¼ cup [35 g] roasted, unsalted whole peanuts

8 dates, pitted

2 Tbsp whole cumin seeds

2 Tbsp whole Sichuan peppercorns

Cilantro leaves and stems, roughly chopped, for garnishing

Sprinkle the lamb chops all over with salt and let stand for up to 1 hour at room temperature or up to overnight in the refrigerator.

Preheat the oven to 425°F [220°C].

Toss the red onion with 1 tablespoon of the olive oil. Place two peanuts in the center of each date, then smush the date halves back together to seal. Using a sheet of aluminum foil, make a packet: Arrange the red onion slices in the center of the foil, then place the peanut-stuffed dates on top and fold the foil over to make a sealed packet. Pop this into the oven, directly onto the rack, while you prep the lamb, for about 10 minutes—it gives the onions a chance to soften up without overcooking.

In a small dry pan over medium-low heat, toast the cumin and the Sichuan peppercorns, stirring continuously to prevent burning, until fragrant and lightly browned, 3 to 4 minutes. Remove from the heat, then add a generous pinch of salt and use a mortar and pestle or a spice grinder to grind into a powder.

Evenly and generously coat the lamb chops with the spice rub, paying particular attention to the fatty bits. In an ovenproof cast-iron pan over medium heat, warm the remaining 1 tablespoon of olive oil. Working in batches if needed, add the lamb chops in a single layer and sear for about 3 minutes per side, or until appetizingly golden brown,

whichever comes first. Do not neglect the fatty seam at the edge of each chop—balance them on their sides to make sure this area browns as well.

Extract your foil packet from the oven, but leave the oven on.

Transfer the lamb chops to a plate. Add ½ cup [120 ml] of water to the pan and deglaze, scraping up any browned bits from the bottom. Remove from the heat, then tip in the onion and dates, along with any oniony juices that may have accumulated in the packet. Arrange the lamb chops on top of this joyous tangle and slide the pan into the oven. Roast for 8 minutes, then flip and roast about 5 minutes longer, or until just medium-rare. Remove from the oven and let rest for 10 minutes before serving.

Crush the remaining peanuts into a coarse rubble (if you used a mortar and pestle to grind the spices earlier, don't bother washing it out in between). Scatter the peanuts and cilantro over the lamb and serve right away.

ANCIENT ROMAN. BRAISED FLAMINGO

SCALD the FLAMINGO, WASH and DRESS iT, PUT iT iN A POT, ADD WATER, SALT, DiLL, and a LITTLE VINEGAR, to be PARBOiLED. FiNiSH COOKiNG WiTH a BUNCH of LEEKS and CORiANDER, and ADD SOME REDUCED MUST to GiVE iT COLOR. iN the MORTAR CRUSH PEPPER, CUMiN, CORiANDER, LASER ROOT, MiNT, RVE, MOiSTEN with VINEGAR, ADD DATES, AND the FOND of the BRAiSED BiRD, THiCKEN, STRAiN, COVER the BiRD with the SAUCE and SERVE. PARROT is PREPARED in the SAME MANNER.

from DE RE COQUINARIA ("The Art of Cooking") by APICIUS— the only surviving cook book of the GRECO-ROMAN ERA.

13-HOUR LAMB WITH DATE & FETA RELISH

DINNER FOR 4 TO 6

The title says 13 hours, but honestly, you could pull this lamb from the oven at any point after hour five and it will be delicious. The idea is that you stick it in there and putter around paying almost zero attention to it—flipping it once every hour or two—until it is completely tender and yielding. Sometimes I like to cook it at higher heat for less time in order to enjoy the slight resistance of the meat against the soft brioche and melty feta relish. Other times, I let it go as long as possible, aiming for lamb so soft you can prod it with a spoon and watch it fall apart. In any case, this is not a recipe to make when you're in a hurry.

At 250°F [120°C], the lamb will take anywhere from 8 to 13 hours.

At 350°F [180°C], the lamb will take anywhere from 3 to 7 hours.

There are no wrong decisions. There is only time.

The lamb is deliberately very savory, in contrast to the salty-sweet relish. If you let it cool completely in its braising liquid, you'll find that the collagen-enriched broth has jellied by morning. This is good, this is gold.

1 bone-in lamb shoulder, about 3 lbs [1.4 kg]

Salt

Freshly ground black pepper

¼ cup [60 ml] olive oil

1 medium onion, halved and peeled

1 head garlic, halved across its equator

1 large carrot, peeled and cut into large chunks

2 celery ribs, cut into large chunks

4 cups [945 ml] beef, chicken, or vegetable broth

6 thyme sprigs

Brioche burger buns, flaky sea salt, fresh lime juice, and Date, Feta & Lavender Relish (page 249), for serving

Preheat the oven to 250°F [120°C] or 350°F [180°C] if you're "in a hurry."

Generously season the lamb with salt and pepper. In a heavy-bottom, ovenproof pot that has a tight-fitting lid and is large enough to snugly hold the lamb shoulder, warm the olive oil over medium-high heat. Sear the lamb until golden brown on all sides, 3 to 4 minutes per side. You might not get complete coverage; just do what you can. Remove the lamb from the pot and set it aside.

Toss the onion, garlic, carrot, and celery into the pot and sear to get some color on them. Add 1 to 2 cups [240 to 475 ml] of the broth and deglaze the pot, scraping up any browned bits from the bottom. Return the lamb to the pot and add the thyme sprigs. Add more broth,

if needed, until the lamb is about two-thirds covered in liquid. You may not need all the broth, or you may need to top it up with water.

Cover the pot and slide it into the oven. Every hour or so, pay the lamb a visit and give it a gentle poke or two and flip it around so that each side has its opportunity to soak up the warm scented broth bath. Continue cooking for at least 3 hours and up to 13 hours. The lamb is done when you can shred it directly in the pot with a regular table fork—butter-tender. Or, it is done whenever you want to eat it after about hour 5. You can serve the lamb right away, or let it cool completely in the braising liquid, then shred it and rewarm the shredded meat on a piping hot, oil-slicked skillet, so you get some good crispy bits. Whatever you do, don't discard the broth; chill and defat it, then use it to make a batch of beans or a sensational noodle soup.

To serve, toast the brioche buns. Layer a goodly quantity of lamb on the bottom buns, then drizzle with just enough warm broth to moisten the meat. Top with a sprinkle of flaky salt and a squeeze of fresh lime juice. Mound with the relish and top with the remaining toasted bun halves. Eat with pickles alongside, or a tangy slaw.

LAMB & PUMPKIN PASTA

DEEP DINNER BOWLS FOR 4, WITH LEFTOVERS

A big cozy bowl of pasta. Here, as elsewhere in the book, the dates and the pumpkin are in constant conversation. You can substitute beef for the lamb, if you like. I've also made a delicious vegetarian variation using assertively browned diced mushrooms that somehow tastes even more autumnal than the lamb version.

3 Tbsp olive oil

1 lb [450 g] ground lamb

2 medium yellow onions, diced

2 medium carrots, diced

1 celery rib, diced

4 garlic cloves, peeled and thinly sliced

One 16 oz [450 g] can pumpkin purée

2 large or 3 small dates, chopped

2 cups [470 ml] water or stock (if stock, you may need less salt)

1 cup [235 ml] milk

1 Tbsp crushed dried oregano

1 tsp red pepper flakes

1 tsp sweet smoked paprika

½ tsp fennel seeds

Salt

Freshly ground black pepper

1 lb [450 g] pasta, preferably mezzi rigatoni

Grated Parmesan cheese, a hit of your best olive oil, some optional but recommended date molasses, and flaky salt, for finishing

In a large, deep pan over medium-high heat, warm 2 tablespoons of the olive oil. Add the ground lamb and cook, using a wooden spoon to break apart any large clumps, for 8 to 10 minutes, or until browned and slightly crispy but not burnt. Don't worry if the lamb releases a lot of liquid; keep cooking and it will resolve itself. Transfer the lamb to a large bowl and set it aside; do not clean the pan.

Adjust the heat to medium-low, then add the onions, carrots, and celery and cook, sweating the vegetables and stirring frequently until soft and opaque but not browned, about 10 minutes. Stir in the garlic slices and cook until fragrant, just a minute or so. Transfer the vegetables to the bowl with the lamb; do not clean the pan.

Turn the heat back up to medium-high and swirl in the remaining 1 tablespoon of olive oil. Spread the pumpkin purée across the entire surface of the hot pan and cook, stirring if needed to expose as much of the pumpkin purée to the pan as possible and trying to get it to

lightly caramelize—you are cooking off some of its excess water and breaking the pumpkin's rawness—about 4 minutes. Add the dates and stir well, then add the water or stock and deglaze the pan, scraping up any browned bits from the bottom. Stir in the lamb, vegetables, milk, oregano, red pepper flakes, paprika, and fennel seeds and season with salt and pepper. Cover, turn the heat to low, and very gently simmer for about 45 minutes. A good indicator of doneness at this point is that the lamb fat forms a slight golden sheen on the surface, having separated during cooking. Taste and season with salt and pepper if needed.

Meanwhile, bring a large pot of generously salted water to a boil over high heat. Add the pasta and cook until al dente, 1 to 2 minutes less than the cooking time on the box. Reserve about 1 cup [240 ml] of the pasta cooking water, then drain the pasta. Stir the pasta into the sauce, adding pasta water about ¼ cup [60 ml] at a time, until the pasta and sauce come together. Serve with grated Parmesan, a drizzle of olive oil, a drizzle of date molasses, a sprinkle of flaky salt and a generous grind of black pepper. Leftovers will keep, tightly covered in the refrigerator, for about 3 days.

SPEEDY, SPICY SHRIMP WITH CHILLED CLEMENTINES

WEEKNIGHT DINNER FOR 4, WITH SIDES (MULTIPLIES EASILY)

This is so quick to make: five minutes to assemble, another five to roast, and you're ready to go. Preheating the oven will take longer than anything else. The recipe scales up easily and is the perfect midweek dinner with a bit of ballast on the side—a green salad and a baguette to mop up the shrimpy juices. This is also a treat to serve at a party as a fancy take on shrimp cocktail: Zhuzh up store-bought cocktail sauce with clementine zest and juice before passing around.

5 clementines

1 Tbsp date molasses

1 garlic clove, grated with a Microplane or very finely minced

¼ tsp red pepper flakes

¼ tsp salt

Freshly ground black pepper

1 lb [450 g] cleaned and shelled shrimp (tail-on is fine)

2 Tbsp very cold butter, cut into tiny cubes

Preheat the oven to 500°F [260°C].
    Peel and segment four of the clementines and chill in the refrigerator or freezer until ready to serve. You want them as cold as possible without being frozen. Zest and juice the remaining clementine. In a large bowl, combine the clementine zest and juice, date molasses, garlic, red pepper flakes, salt, and a generous grind of pepper. Add the shrimp and toss until fully coated.

    Spread the shrimp out in a single layer on a rimmed baking sheet. Dot each shrimp with a cube of butter and slide into the oven for about 5 minutes. Keep an eye on the shrimp—you want to pull them just as they start to turn beautifully pink and opaque and before their edges start to curl. Serve straight from the oven with the cold cold cold chilled clementine slices to contrast with the hot buttery shrimp.

TANGY SESAME SHRIMP

DINNER FOR 4, WITH SIDES

A quick weeknight meal that nevertheless feels special. There are a couple of useful tricks here: a 15-minute brine in a very little bit of baking soda improves the shrimp's texture, keeping it bouncy, firm, and crisp, even after cooking. Baking soda also helps to break down the date flesh, so it is doing double duty (that's why a baking soda soak is often a step in sticky toffee pudding, for instance).

These shrimp cook fast, so make sure you have everything ready to go before you turn on the heat.

8 barhi or other semisoft dates

5 Tbsp [80 ml] hot-but-not-boiling water

1 lb [450 g] shell-on shrimp

¼ tsp baking soda

1 tsp salt

2 tsp soy sauce

2 tsp fish sauce

1 tsp apple cider vinegar

½ tsp roasted sesame oil

½ tsp sugar (or date molasses, if you have any handy)

1 Tbsp grapeseed or other neutral oil

Lime wedges, to squeeze over when serving

Pit the dates and soak them in a small bowl filled with the hot water. Set aside.

Brine the shrimp: In a medium nonreactive bowl, toss the shrimp with the baking soda and salt and set to rest in the refrigerator for 15 minutes. Leave the shells on the shrimp to trap the sauce; you can peel them at table or eat shell-on for a bit of a calcium boost.

Meanwhile, use a fork or your fingers to mash the dates in the warm water until you have a thick, creamy liquid. Pull out the shrimp and toss them in the date mixture. Set them to rest in the refrigerator for another 15 minutes.

To make the sauce, in a medium bowl, combine the soy sauce, fish sauce, vinegar, sesame oil, and sugar and stir until the sugar is dissolved.

To cook the shrimp, in a large sauté pan, skillet, or wok over medium heat, warm the grapeseed oil. Tip in the marinated shrimp and sauté until they lose their translucency, firm up, and start to turn pink. Tip in the sauce and continue cooking until the mixture starts to caramelize, just a minute or two, then dish up and serve with lime wedges alongside. This is delicious with

coconut rice or plain basmati rice to soak up the tangy sauce, and is best eaten on the day it's made.

MISO—MUSTARD SALMON & ASPARAGUS

A LIGHT DINNER FOR 4, WITH SIDES

For that springtime moment when the asparagus looks good, but nothing else has caught up. Look for slender asparagus spears so they cook in roughly the same time as the fish. You can, of course, try this at other times of year with other vegetables, such as eggplant or zucchini. You can also use steelhead trout or another similar fish instead of salmon—just look for something mild and sweet that will complement the dates in the marinade. If you don't have malt vinegar, try something else tangy and light, such as apple cider vinegar. The malt vinegar lends the dish a real fish and chips vibe, which is why I like it here.

4 skin-on salmon fillets, about 6 oz [170 g] each

Salt

Freshly ground black pepper

3 dates, pitted, roughly chopped, and soaked in 2 Tbsp of warm water

1 fat garlic clove, grated with a Microplane or very finely minced

2 Tbsp olive oil

2 Tbsp Dijon mustard

1 Tbsp white (shiro) miso

1 Tbsp malt vinegar

1 lb [450 g] asparagus, woody ends snapped off

Generously sprinkle the salmon fillets all over with salt and pepper.

In a small bowl, combine the mushy dates and their soaking water with the garlic, olive oil, mustard, miso, and malt vinegar, stirring until blended.

Pour about half of this marinade on top of the salmon fillets and gently smoosh the fish around until evenly coated. Let the fish marinate in the refrigerator for 15 to 30 minutes. Toss the asparagus spears in the remaining marinade and set aside until ready to cook.

Preheat the oven to 325°F [165°C]. Line a rimmed baking sheet with parchment paper.

Place the salmon fillets, skin-side down, on the prepared baking sheet and surround with the asparagus spread out in a single layer. Bake until the salmon is just opaque and gently flakes when pressed with a fork, 15 to 20 minutes. If either the fish or asparagus is looking a little pale and lackluster at this point, turn the broiler on high (stay close, the marinade burns easily) until everything becomes a little more golden. Serve with grains or greens or both to round out the meal.

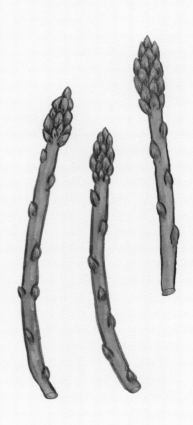

KUWAITI RED SNAPPER WITH ONION RICE

DINNER FOR 4, WITH RICE

The traditional version of this dish uses a whole red snapper, stuffed and encased in a bright, turmeric-forward spiced date paste and grilled over hot coals. The date paste seals in the fish's juices and keeps the flesh moist and tender. I've adapted the recipe to be more weeknight friendly, using snapper fillets and an oven. If you can't find snapper, any mild and flaky fish, such as cod, grouper, sea bass, rockfish, or tilapia, will work. If you can, get your fishmonger to give you the snapper as a whole slab—instead of individual fillets, a single 2 lb [910 g] piece is ideal. The fish is best served with Onion Rice (recipe follows), a traditional accompaniment for seafood.

I first encountered a version of this recipe in *The Arab Table: Recipes and Culinary Traditions* by May S. Bsisu. My copy is more than twenty years old, splattered and stained and marked up with notes. It has been an invaluable kitchen companion and is my favorite recommendation for anyone in the United States who is looking for an introduction to cooking Middle Eastern food. For this recipe, Bsisu recommends dry-textured Golden Zahidi dates, with their notes of bread and caramel. If you can't find them, Sukkari dates are a more readily available substitute.

See the Hot Date! Pantry (page 38) for more about loomi, or dried Omani limes.

25 Sukkari or Golden Zahidi dates, pitted
1 large yellow onion, finely chopped
6 garlic cloves, grated with a Microplane, minced, or mashed to a paste with a mortar and pestle
1 jalapeño, finely chopped (optional)
1 cup [12 g] packed chopped cilantro
¼ cup [5 g] chopped fresh dill
1 Tbsp salt
1 Tbsp coarsely ground white pepper
1 Tbsp ground turmeric
1 tsp ground ginger
1 loomi or black lime, grated into a powder or crushed with a mortar and pestle or spice grinder (or 1½ tsp ground loomi powder)
1 Tbsp olive oil
4 red snapper fillets or 1 large slab, about 2 lbs [910 g] total

In a medium bowl, soak the dates in lukewarm water for 10 to 15 minutes.

In a large bowl, thoroughly combine the onion, garlic, jalapeño (if using), cilantro, dill, salt, white pepper, turmeric, ginger, and grated loomi.

Drain the dates, then mash them into a paste using a potato masher, a wooden spoon, or by just squeezing them with your hands until gooey. Using a large wooden spoon, work the date paste and olive oil into the onion and herb mixture. You may need to add a little water to thin out the date paste enough for everything to mix together, but don't overdo it—the paste should be thick enough to coat the fish without sliding off.

Rub a thick layer of the date paste all over the fish so it's completely encased. (Wear surgical gloves to do this if you're worried about staining your hands yellow with turmeric.) Put the fish in the refrigerator to marinate for 3 hours.

If grilling, cook the fish in a clamshell grate over indirect heat. If using the oven, put the fish on a parchment paper–lined rimmed baking sheet and bake at 400°F [200°C]. Cook until the fish's flesh shifts from translucent to just opaque and flakes when prodded gently with a fork, 20 to 30 minutes; the internal temperature should be 145°F [62°C]. The date paste shell may be charred in places. Don't worry, it's still delicious. Serve with onion rice (recipe follows).

ONION RICE

2 cups [400 g] basmati rice

¼ cup [60 ml] olive oil

2 large yellow onions, finely chopped

1 tsp salt

1 tsp ground turmeric

1 tsp ground cumin

1 tsp ground coriander

1 tsp ground cinnamon

½ tsp ground allspice

½ tsp freshly ground black pepper

In a medium bowl, rinse the rice and drain. Refill the water and leave the rice to soak while you complete the next steps.

In a large, heavy-bottom pot with a tight-fitting lid, heat the olive oil over medium heat. Add the onions and cook, stirring to prevent burning, until softened and starting to darken at the edges, about 7 minutes. Turn the heat to low, then add the salt, turmeric, cumin, coriander, cinnamon, allspice, and pepper. Cook, stirring continuously, until the spices are just fragrant, less than 1 minute. Drain the rice and add the grains to the pot, stirring to fully coat them in the oil and spices. Add 2 cups [475 ml] of water and bring to a boil over high heat, then turn the heat as low as possible, cover, and cook for 20 minutes, or until all the liquid is gone

and the rice is tender and fluffy. You should be able to see the long grains of rice sticking up like fish poking their heads out of the water. Remove from the heat and let the rice rest, covered, for at least 10 minutes.

Taste the rice. If it tastes bland or watered-down, sprinkle a generous pinch of salt over it, fluff the rice with a fork, and pop the lid back on for 2 to 3 minutes off the heat to allow the grains to absorb the salt. This rice will really sing against seafood if it's properly salted, but be careful not to overcorrect and oversalt.

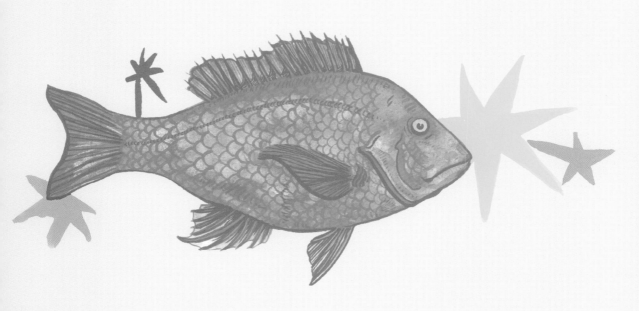

BROWN BUTTER SCALLOPS

A LIGHT MAIN FOR 4, WITH SIDES (MULTIPLIES EASILY)

With an unexpected rose-flecked flavor that plays off the natural sweetness of the scallops, this elegant supper is mellow, rounded, and complex. The date sugar adds a textural je ne sais quoi.

The recipe scales up easily and makes a fun passed appetizer at a party. Ask your fishmonger if they've got any scallop shells you can have; each shell can be used as a little plate for a memorable hors d'oeuvre.

If you have any of the walnut sprinkle left over, it makes for great popcorn, or an alternative topping to your regular cinnamon-sugar toast.

12 dry jumbo sea scallops

2 Tbsp roughly crushed raw walnuts, the consistency of wet sand

2 tsp coarse date sugar

1 tsp crushed dried organic rose petals

½ tsp ground cinnamon

Big pinch of salt

1 to 2 Tbsp ghee or neutral cooking oil

4 Tbsp [55 g] butter

1 Tbsp fresh lemon juice

Thoroughly pat dry the scallops and put them, uncovered, in the refrigerator while you prep the rest of the ingredients.

In a small bowl, combine the walnuts, date sugar, rose petals, cinnamon, and salt. Set aside.

In a large, heavy-bottom skillet over medium heat, warm 1 tablespoon of the ghee or oil. Working in batches if needed to avoid crowding the pan, gently add the scallops to the skillet in a single layer and cook for 4 to 6 minutes, or until golden brown on the bottom. Flip the scallops and cook for a maximum of 2 more minutes, or until just golden on the other side. Don't crowd the pan and don't overcook the scallops. Transfer the scallops to a serving platter; do not clean the skillet.

Sprinkle a generous mounded dose of the walnut mixture on top of each scallop. Keep warm.

In the still-hot skillet, melt the butter and swirl it around until it starts to brown. When it is decisively dark and nutty-smelling but not yet burnt, stir in the lemon juice and quickly spoon the mixture over the scallops, being sure to hit the walnut mixture with the hot fragrant butter to release both flavors and aromas. Serve immediately.

JUST OUTSIDE RIYADH, in the KING-DOM of SAUDI ARABIA

FIVE THOUSAND FRUITING DATE PALMS

A VISIT to a DATE "FARM" PLANTED
for a PRINCE — WE WERE TAKEN ON AN AMBLE
THROUGH the GROVE at DUSK, 5,000 PALMS
SWAYING in the BREEZE. THE ORCHARD SOMETHI
BETWEEN A WORKING FARM & a WEEKEND
RETREAT, the TREES DRAMATICALLY LIT, SPOT-
LIGHTS CASTING PALM FROND SHADOWS ACROSS ou
PATH. TINY BATS SKITTERING THROUGH the
GLOAMING. COURTYARDS & A WINDTOWER-
COOLED MAJLIS, & A FIREPIT TO STAVE OFF
the EVENING CHILL of the DESERT AIR.
WE WERE GIVEN A FEAST, A WHOLE LAMB
STEWED in YOGURT ON A FRAGRANT BED of RICE,
ALL the FIXINGS. TWO BOTTLES of LABAN-UP AT
EVERY PLACE SETTING, & A BOTTLE of TABASCO
EACH — the NECESSARY ACCOUTREMENTS. FOR
DESSERT, DEEP SAUCERS of FUDGY BATHEETH
CRUMBLE, A TRADITIONAL REGIONAL SWEET
MADE WITH DATES from the FARM, COOKED
DOWN with TOASTED WHEAT FLOUR and
ALMOST OVERWHELMING QUANTITIES of
SAFFRON AND CARDAMOM, TINY CUPS
of GAHWA to FINISH.

BATHEETH

SOUPS, SALADS & SIDES

DOUBLE-GINGER CARROT SOUP

SOUP FOR 4

A straightforward and weeknight-friendly soup, with the dates coaxing out the inherent sweetness of the carrots. The plush, velvety texture of this soup is the mealtime equivalent of a warm blanket. Add a little oomph with a spoonful of Spiced Date Chili Crisp (page 244), or serve alongside a Date & Kashkaval Grilled Cheese (page 59) for a very soothing meal indeed.

2 Tbsp olive oil or coconut oil, plus more for serving

1 large leek, white and pale green parts only, washed and roughly chopped

1 thumb-size piece fresh ginger, peeled and chopped

3 garlic cloves, chopped

2 lbs [910 g] carrots, washed and roughly chopped into coins

6 dates, pitted and roughly chopped, plus more chopped dates for serving

1 tsp ground ginger

½ tsp ground cinnamon

One 14 oz [415 ml] can coconut milk

About 3½ cups [830 ml] chicken or vegetable stock or water

Salt

Freshly ground black pepper

Crème fraiche/yogurt/labneh, chopped cilantro or mint, toasted pepitas or sunflower seeds, fresh lime juice, and/or your favorite chili crunch, for serving

In a large, deep pot over medium heat, warm the olive or coconut oil until shimmering. Add the leek and sauté until just starting to soften and turn translucent, 2 to 3 minutes. Add the fresh ginger, followed by the garlic, and cook until pale golden brown. Add the carrots and dates and stir to coat everything in the oil. Add the ground ginger and cinnamon, stir to incorporate, and when everything is hot and fragrant, stir in the coconut milk to deglaze the pan, scraping up any browned bits from the bottom. Add two cans-worth of stock or water (about 3½ cups [830 ml]) and bring to a boil. Lower the heat to a simmer and cook until the carrots are soft and have turned the oils in the coconut milk a beautiful yellow-orange, 20 to 25 minutes. Using an immersion blender, blend the soup in the pot until aerated and smooth. (If you don't have an immersion blender, you can use a regular blender; work in batches and be careful, as the soup is very hot.) Taste and season with salt and pepper if needed.

Serve with any or all of the suggestions in the ingredients list; you are looking to add a bit of tangy creaminess (labneh, yogurt, crème frâiche), a bit of crunch (nuts and seeds), a bit of heat (chili crunch), and a bit of brightness (fresh herbs, citrus juice). The soup will keep in the refrigerator for up to 5 days and up to 2 months in the freezer.

RED LENTIL SOUP WITH A DATE MOLASSES DRIZZLE

SOUP FOR 4

This is comfort in a bowl, the soup I would eat every day if I could (and, at some points in time, I have). Is the drizzle of date molasses strictly traditional or necessary? No. But it makes the spices sing and adds a note of indulgence to an otherwise homely, no-frills bowl of joy.

2 Tbsp olive oil, plus more for serving

1 medium onion, chopped

2 cups [400 g] red lentils, picked over, rinsed, and drained

1 medium tomato, chopped

8 cups [1.9 L] chicken stock or water

1½ Tbsp ground cumin

1 tsp salt

½ tsp white pepper

Date molasses, lemon wedges, radish slices, olives, fresh mint leaves, fresh pitas charred briefly over a stovetop flame or toasted in the oven, for serving

In a large, deep pot over medium heat, warm the olive oil until shimmering. Add the onion and sauté until soft and translucent at the edges but not browned, about 5 minutes. Add the lentils and stir to coat them with the olive oil. Stir in the chopped tomato, followed by the stock or water and bring to a boil. Turn the heat to medium-low and simmer gently until the lentils are soft, 15 to 30 minutes. Skim off and discard any scum that rises to the surface.

Once the lentils are soft, shower the cumin, salt, and white pepper over them. Using an immersion blender, blend the soup in the pot until silky and full-bodied. (If you don't have an immersion blender, you can use a regular blender; work in batches and be careful, as the soup is very hot.) Bring the soup back to a boil, then turn the heat to low and simmer for 15 minutes. Taste and season with salt and pepper if needed; you may need more salt if you used water rather than stock.

Ladle the soup into bowls and drizzle each with about ½ tablespoon of date molasses and a goodly pour of olive oil. Serve with lemon wedges and let each diner finish their own bowl with radishes, olives, and mint leaves. The pitas are welcome companions either torn and tossed into the soup or dipped in for more measured bites. This soup makes for exceptional leftovers and improves in flavor over time. It will keep in the refrigerator for up to 5 days and in the freezer for up to 2 months. Be aware that it will thicken to a cement-like stodge as it rests, so you may need to cut it with water (and additional salt, if needed) to thin it back out as you reheat it.

YELLOW BARHI & GREEN APPLE KALE SALAD

SALAD FOR 4

A salad to make if you are suffering from an embarrassment of fresh dates, when they are in the crisp-tender khalal stage. In the United States, Barhi dates are the variety most commonly sold like this—for a few brief weeks in late summer and early fall, you can find glowing yellow orbs at Middle Eastern grocery stores or online, shipped directly from the Coachella Valley (see the Where to Shop section on page 260 for advice on where to order some). The combination of sweet-crispy dates and tart-crunchy apple makes for a lovely it's-almost-autumn-but-it's-still-too-hot-to-turn-on-my-oven salad. If you'd like to eat this salad at any other time of year, you can use regular tamar-stage dates—just check to see if you need to dial up the salt or lemon juice to counteract the additional sweetness.

4 cups [60 g] finely chopped kale

3 Tbsp fresh lemon juice

Salt

Freshly ground black pepper

3 Tbsp olive oil

2 oz [55 g] sharp, crumbly Cheddar cheese, diced

1 tart green apple, diced

10 to 15 yellow Barhi or other khalal-stage dates, pitted and quartered

¼ cup [30 g] pecan halves, toasted and cooled

1 garlic clove, grated with a Microplane or very finely minced

In a large salad bowl, drizzle the kale with 1 tablespoon of the lemon juice, a big pinch (about ¼ teaspoon) of salt, and a good grind or two of pepper. Vigorously massage the kale, rubbing in the salt, pepper, and lemon juice to break down the fibrous leaves. Once they are glistening and well-scrunched, drizzle in about 1 tablespoon of the olive oil and lock the salt and citrus in with another tough-love massage. Add the Cheddar, apple, dates, and pecans and toss to combine.

In a small bowl, whisk together the remaining 2 tablespoons of lemon juice, the remaining 2 tablespoons of olive oil, the garlic, another big pinch of salt, and more black pepper. Add to the salad bowl and toss well. Let stand about 15 minutes, then finesse with salt and pepper one more time before serving. If you wait to add the apples until just before serving, all the other components of the salad will keep for at least 1 day, possibly 2, in the refrigerator.

MIDSUMMER SALAD

SALAD FOR 2 TO 4

This is one of my favorite ways to take down a bunch of high summer produce in one go. Blanching the green beans and corn kernels not only keeps them snappy, it warms them up just enough to deeply absorb the mustardy dressing. The longer the salad sits, the more pickled the vegetables get. You can substitute a tablespoon of date molasses for the whole date in the dressing; just know that you need something sweet to smooth out the edges of the vinegar and play off the earthy walnut oil.

For a real treat, spoon the "whiskey"— the vibrant umami-laced combination of dressing and juices that collects at the bottom of the salad bowl—into ice-filled shot glasses and serve alongside the meal for your guests to sip on.

1 large date, pitted and finely diced

2 Tbsp red wine vinegar

¼ cup [60 ml] walnut oil or olive oil

1 Tbsp Dijon mustard

Salt

Freshly ground black pepper

1 lb [450 g] green beans, topped and tailed

2 ears sweet corn, kernels cut off cobs

8 oz [225 g] cherry tomatoes, halved

1 medium or ½ large red onion, diced

5 or 6 fresh basil leaves, roughly torn

In a large bowl, submerge the chopped date in the red wine vinegar. Set aside to loosen up for a few minutes, then whisk in the walnut oil and mustard until emulsified and creamy. Add a generous pinch of salt and several grinds of pepper. The dressing should be very bright from the vinegar and mustard and sweet with pops of date flesh. Set aside.

Bring a large pot of salted water to a boil. Set a large bowl of ice water next to your sink.

When the water is at a rolling boil, add the green beans and corn kernels and blanch for 2 minutes or less (the beans should be bright green and alert, nowhere close to mushy), then drain and immediately plunge into the bowl of ice water. Swish the vegetables around until they're just cool; you want to stop them cooking but not chill them all the way. Drain again and pat dry, then toss into the large bowl with the dressing. Mix thoroughly, then add the cherry tomatoes, red onion, and torn basil. Toss everything together so it's coated in the dressing, then taste and finesse with salt and pepper if needed.

You can serve this salad immediately or let it sit for 30 minutes or so at room temperature for the flavors to acclimate to each other. It's an assertive salad and should taste punchy and bright and like you want to keep going back in and picking at it. The salad is good the next day if stored in an airtight container in the refrigerator, but it will taste slightly more pickled—never a problem in our house.

FENNEL RIBBONS WITH SALTY PEANUTS

SALAD FOR 4, AS A SIDE

Featherlight wisps of fennel are tossed with a rubble of deeply toasted peanuts and a slick of date molasses in this slightly weird but very tasty dish. Shaving and then salting root vegetables is one of my favorite methods for turning a hard and gnarly thing you pulled out of the ground into an ethereal side. This salad makes a lovely complement to a joint of meat or big roasted mushrooms but is also delicate enough to serve with fish. So simple! So nuanced! So yummy!

If you can only find salted peanuts, wait to add the second pinch of salt until after you've dressed the fennel with the molasses and toasted nut rubble and tasted it to be sure you need more.

1 large fennel bulb

About ½ tsp salt

⅓ cup [50 g] unsalted skin-on raw or roasted whole peanuts

1 tsp olive oil

1 Tbsp date molasses

Using a mandoline or Y-shaped vegetable peeler, shave the fennel as thinly as possible. Put it in a large bowl, add a big pinch of salt, and toss thoroughly. Set aside for 5 to 10 minutes while you tend to the peanuts.

If you are using already roasted peanuts, crush them with a mortar and pestle or pulse them in a food processor until they are a coarse rubble (not a paste—we're not looking for peanut butter here). Add the olive oil and another big pinch of salt and stir until thoroughly combined.

If you are using raw peanuts, crush as above. In a medium skillet over medium heat, warm the olive oil. Add the peanuts and toast, stirring continuously, until deep golden brown but not burnt, about 3 minutes. Pull the peanuts from the heat a little earlier than you think you need to, as they'll keep browning. Stir in a big pinch of salt and set aside to cool slightly.

Toss the fennel with the date molasses and the peanuts until completely coated and serve immediately.

CARROT & CUMIN SALAD

SALAD FOR 2, WHEN IT IS NEEDED THE MOST

Every cook needs a reset button in her arsenal, and this is the one I turn to time and again. After extended bouts of Too Much—too much fun, too many festive meals, too much takeout, too much work stress—my spouse and I will find ourselves spontaneously turning to each other and saying, "Carrot salad? Carrot salad!" There's some alchemy that happens when carrots, cumin, and dates combine. I can't explain it. Maybe you can.

If need be, this can be stretched into a proper meal with the addition of some ballast—a can of chickpeas, some feta—but I find its powers most formidable when it is left in its purest form. When I have the wherewithal, I grate the carrots into ultrafine shreds using a Microplane, turning the salad's texture into something almost like shaved ice, dissolving on the tongue. Finally: Yes, you can use pre-ground cumin, but I promise it's worth the extra few minutes of effort to coax out the musky, earthy tang of the whole seeds.

1 tsp whole cumin seeds
¼ tsp ground coriander
¼ tsp ground cinnamon
¼ tsp mild red chili flakes, such as Aleppo or Urfa biber
½ tsp sugar

½ tsp salt
½ tsp freshly ground black pepper
1½ Tbsp fresh lemon juice (about 1 small lemon)
1 Tbsp olive oil
1 lb [450 g] carrots, peeled and grated
6 dates, pitted and diced
1 Tbsp finely chopped fresh flat-leaf parsley

Put the cumin in a small cold skillet or sauté pan and set it over medium heat. Toast, stirring frequently, until the cumin is emphatically fragrant but not burnt, no more than a few minutes. Transfer the cumin to a mortar and pestle or a spice grinder and grind to a powder. Tip the ground cumin into a large bowl, then add the coriander, cinnamon, chili flakes, sugar, salt, and pepper. Stir in the lemon juice and olive oil, then add the carrots, dates, and parsley and toss to thoroughly combine. Let rest in the refrigerator for at least 2 hours so the flavors can mingle. The salad will be just as good, if not better, the next day if stored overnight in an airtight container in the refrigerator.

ROASTED CARROTS WITH DATE BUTTER

SIDE FOR 6

These carrots are oven-steamed in a water, butter, and date molasses solution, then drained and roasted into sticky, caramelized batons. The date molasses intensifies the sweetness of the carrots, while the carrots tint the butter a glorious sunset orange and lend a mellow earthiness to the molasses; all is reduced to an unctuous glaze that coats everything in the purest essence of carrot.

Leftover carrots make an unusual but delicious sandwich. Lavishly butter the inside of a baguette, then pile in the tender, sticky carrots and top with a fistful of arugula and thick planks of hard goat cheese. Finish with a slick of mustard, then compress the sandwich slightly—to get the carrots properly smooshed—and eat.

1 cup [50 g] very finely chopped fresh chives and/or dill

Salt

2 Tbsp date molasses

Freshly ground black pepper

2 Tbsp butter, cut into small pieces

1 tsp whole cumin seeds

2 lbs [910 g] carrots, scrubbed and halved lengthwise if large

2 Tbsp olive oil

Labneh or crème fraîche

Preheat the oven to 450°F [230°C].

In a medium bowl, toss the chives and/or dill with a big pinch (about ¼ teaspoon) of salt. Set aside.

In a deep rimmed baking sheet, stir the date molasses with 1½ cups [360 ml] of water until fully dissolved. Add big pinches of salt and pepper, along with the butter and cumin, then toss the carrots with this mixture until completely coated. Cover the pan tightly with aluminum foil and steam in the oven for about 30 minutes, or until the carrots are tender when pierced with a knife. Leave the oven on.

Drain the liquid into a large skillet and set over medium heat. Cook, stirring if needed, until reduced by about half. The butter droplets should have taken on a marigold cast from the carrots.

Meanwhile, on a rimmed baking sheet, toss the carrots with the olive oil and roast, uncovered, for about 20 minutes, or until golden brown and slightly caramelized.

To serve, paint a thick swoosh of labneh or crème fraîche on a platter, then jenga a stack of carrots on top. Drizzle liberally with the reduced glaze and top with a shower of salted herbs. These carrots are best eaten the day they are made.

PUY LENTIL SALAD WITH SMOKED DUCK

SALAD FOR 4

There is something very pleasing about the combination of lentils, mustard, and walnut oil. Earthy, nutty, smooth, sweet. This is the sort of lunch salad that gets better with time; make a big batch and keep it in the refrigerator for meals all week. It's very texturally varied, filled with crunchy root vegetables and little pops of bright briny flavor from the dates and olives. This salad is also accommodating of other ingredients. Try radishes, celery, capers, chopped sun-dried tomatoes, pickled onions, diced cornichons . . . The smoked duck breast is optional but delightful.

1 cup [200 g] French green lentils, preferably du Puy, picked over, rinsed, and drained

2½ cups [600 ml] chicken or vegetable stock or water

¼ cup [60 ml] walnut oil

¼ cup [60 ml] red wine vinegar

1 Tbsp Dijon mustard

1 tsp honey or date molasses

Salt

Freshly ground black pepper

1 large carrot, peeled and diced

1 shallot or small red onion, diced

6 large or 8 small dates, pitted and roughly chopped

8 to 12 oil-cured black olives, pitted and roughly chopped

3 Tbsp roughly chopped fresh flat-leaf parsley

1 ready-to-eat smoked duck breast

In a large pot, combine the lentils and the stock or water and bring to a boil. Turn the heat to medium-low and simmer, uncovered, until the lentils are tender, about 20 minutes. Drain the lentils.

Meanwhile, in a small bowl, whisk together the walnut oil, red wine vinegar, mustard, and honey or date molasses until emulsified. Stir in generous pinches of salt and pepper—the dressing should be assertively tangy and salty, as it is going to flavor the lentils.

While the lentils are still warm, stir in the dressing. Let stand for a few minutes, then taste and season with salt if needed. Stir in the carrot, shallot or red onion, dates, olives, and parsley. Divide between four plates. Thinly slice the smoked duck breast, if using, and drape it over the lentils— allow three or four ⅛ inch [3 mm] thick slices per serving. Duckless, the lentil salad will keep for up to 5 days in the refrigerator, improving with age. Serve at room temperature for optimal texture.

SHAVED CELERY SALAD WITH SPICED DATE CHILI CRISP

SALAD FOR 4, AS A SIDE

Spicy yet cooling! Zingy and filled with vitality! This salad brimmeth o'er with irresistible crunch. Free your celery from a crisper drawer death spiral with this pantry-staple solution, which I happily inhale by the bowlful but is also a worthy foundation to any number of meals: glossed out with mayo as the base for an egg or potato (or shrimp!) salad; spread on a plate to make a verdant carpet for a fried egg (keep the yolk runny, so it can spill out and dress the fiery celery); a side for dumplings; a crunchy topper for rice . . .

2 Tbsp fresh lime juice

1 to 2 Tbsp Spiced Date Chili Crisp (page 244) or your favorite chili crisp

1 Tbsp sesame oil

1 Tbsp soy sauce

Up to ½ tsp sugar

8 celery ribs, cut as thinly as possible, preferably using a mandoline

4 dates, pitted and thinly chopped

Big handful of cilantro leaves

In a large bowl, stir together the lime juice, chili crisp, sesame oil, and soy sauce. Taste and add a touch of sugar if needed to round out the sharpness—the dates in the chili crisp may already provide enough sweetness. Add the celery and dates and toss to coat thoroughly. Let the salad sit for 5 to 10 minutes, then sprinkle with cilantro just before serving. The salad will keep, in an airtight container in the refrigerator, for 2 to 3 days, though it will get spicier over time.

SPICY CHARRED SWEET POTATO PLANKS

SIDE FOR 2

The date molasses here provides a mysterious yet compelling bass note, adding depth and complexity to the natural sugariness of the sweet potato. Combined with the olive oil and turmeric, the molasses bubbles and chars appealingly in a hot oven and creates lacy, caramelized edges as the sweet potato slabs cook. They should end up charred in spots and crispy on the outside yet pudding-soft when you bite in.

1 Tbsp olive oil

1 Tbsp date molasses

½ tsp smoked chili flakes (or regular, if you don't have smoked)

½ tsp ground turmeric

Salt

Freshly ground black pepper

1 large sweet potato, cut into thick steak fry–like planks

Labneh or very thick Greek yogurt, toasted nuts or toasted chickpeas, and lime zest, for serving

Preheat the oven to 425°F [220°C]. Line a rimmed baking sheet with parchment paper.

In a large bowl, combine the olive oil, date molasses, smoked chili flakes, turmeric, and big pinches of salt and pepper. Stir to blend into a paste, then add the sweet potato planks and smush them around to coat every side. Allow to hang out for a brief marination session, around 5 to 10 minutes.

Spread the sweet potatoes out in a single layer on the prepared baking sheet. Make sure they aren't too close together or they will steam and won't get crispy. If there's any marinade left in the bottom of the bowl, pour it directly onto the sweet potatoes. Roast, untouched, for about 30 minutes, or until golden brown and blackened in spots. Flip the sweet potatoes and roast for 5 more minutes to give the reverse side some color. These sweet potatoes are as good at room temperature as they are hot. To serve, smear a swoosh of yogurt that you've doctored with salt and lime zest across the base of a plate and lay the sweet potato planks on top. Scatter with toasted nuts or crispy chickpeas, and serve.

PEAS WITH MINT & PRESERVED LEMON

SIDE FOR 4

Fresh peas, sweet dates, briny lemon—a winning combination. While this dish is at its peak when made with fresh spring peas, you can make it at any time of year using a bag of frozen peas. I like to use firmer dates, like Deglet Nours, in this dish—their slight chew makes for a welcome contrast to the snappy peas.

3 Tbsp butter

2 cups [260 g] green peas

1 Tbsp finely chopped preserved lemon flesh and rind or ½ Tbsp preserved lemon paste

¼ tsp salt

5 dates, pitted and chopped into pea-sized pieces

3 Tbsp finely chopped fresh mint

In a large skillet or sauté pan over medium heat, melt the butter until foaming. Stir in the peas, preserved lemon, and salt, then cover and cook until the peas are bright green and fully warmed through, 3 to 5 minutes. Remove the pan from heat, stir in the dates and mint, and season with additional salt if needed. Serve warm or at room temperature. Leftovers will keep, tightly covered in the refrigerator, for up to 3 days; wait to add the mint until just before you eat if you're planning to keep them for that long.

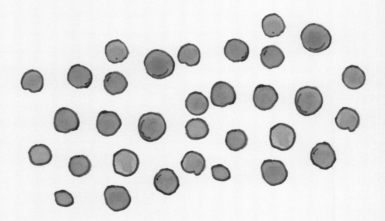

BUTTER-ROASTED RADISHES

SIDE FOR 4

I originally wrote this recipe for spicy spring radishes, and roasting them alongside dates is indeed a delightful way to mellow out their zippy person-alities. However! It is just as pertinent a recipe deep in root vegetable season, when you are staring down a crisper drawer filled with the hardiest speci-mens—a helpful way to tenderize and enliven the most stoic winter nubbins.

If you can only find salt-packed capers, rinse off the salt before you use them. And if you have any preserved lemons lying around—say you used some to make the peas on the facing page, or the Preserved Lemon Gremolata (page 125)— they'd be a welcome addition here, along with or instead of the fresh lemon zest. Be sure to taste for salt first, since the anchovies and capers are already pretty briny.

1 small (2 oz [55 g]) tin olive oil–packed anchovies

Olive oil, if needed

⅓ cup [50 g] chopped dates

3 garlic cloves, grated with a Microplane or very finely minced

3 Tbsp brined capers

Zest and juice of ½ lemon

1 Tbsp butter

2 bunches snappy spring radishes (about 1½ lbs [680 g]), leaves left on if sufficiently perky

½ cup [15 g] chopped fresh flat-leaf parsley

Salt

Freshly ground black pepper

Preheat the oven to 400°F [200°C].

In a large ovenproof skillet or sauté pan over medium heat, melt the anchovies in the oil they came in, stirring with a wooden spoon until they dissolve, about 5 minutes. Add more olive oil if needed. Remove the pan from the heat, then stir in the dates, garlic, capers, lemon zest, and butter. Mix until the butter is glossy and mostly melted. Set aside.

Halve any larger radishes, keep-ing the greens attached if you can. Keep the little radishes whole—you are aiming for all of them to end up roughly the same size, so they roast in the same amount of time.

Add the radishes to the anchovy-caper mixture in the skillet and toss to coat. Spread out the mixture (or transfer it to a rimmed baking sheet if preferred) and roast until the radishes are tender and can be easily speared with a knife, 15 to 20 minutes. Toss with the parsley and lemon juice, season with salt and pepper, and serve warm. This dish is best enjoyed on the day it is made.

RUTAB & SUMMER TOMATOES WITH SIZZLING BROWN BUTTER

STARTER OR SIDE FOR 4, WITH BREAD

A revelatory flavor combination, this recipe has, hands down, the highest reward-to-effort ratio in this book. If you make one recipe, try this one. When dates are harvested in late summer and early fall, they are at what is known as the rutab stage, with flesh that is custard-soft and lush. Where I live in the northeast United States, it's also tomato harvest season, my favorite time of year. This dish is transcendent when made with peak-season rutab dates and summer's finest tomatoes, but you can make it with hydroponic midwinter cherry tomatoes and regular Medjools and still find yourself greedily mopping up the buttery remains.

Use just enough yuzu kosho to add fragrance and a breath of heat without overwhelming the other flavors. If you can't find yuzu kosho, don't let that stop you: This dish is good with just the butter! Sometimes I like to omit the kosho anyway and stir a tablespoon of good red wine vinegar, along with an extra-generous pinch of flaky salt, into the hot butter instead; other times I go with red pepper flakes and lime zest. Not the same, but differently delicious.

12 dates, the softer and more luscious the better

10 oz [285 g] tomatoes

4 Tbsp [55 g] butter

¼ to ½ tsp red yuzu kosho

Flaky salt

Freshly ground black pepper

Bread, for serving

Tear open the dates and remove the pits. Arrange on a serving plate. If using cherry or grape tomatoes, cut them in half. Otherwise, cut the tomatoes so they're roughly the same size and shape as the torn dates. Arrange the tomatoes on the serving plate, cut-side up and interspersed with the dates.

In a small, heavy pan over medium heat, melt the butter. Continue cooking the butter until it starts to darken and sizzle, about 5 minutes. It should smell nutty and fragrant and turn a deep, beautiful caramel brown. Stay close to the pan while doing this; browned butter can go from delicious to burnt in seconds. Immediately remove from the heat. Stir the yuzu kosho into the butter until completely dissolved. Pour the hot butter mixture directly over the dates and tomatoes—they should sizzle! Sprinkle with a big pinch of large-flake salt, like Maldon, and a generous grind of black pepper. Serve with bread to mop everything up.

MUSHROOMS EN PAPILLOTE WITH MUCH GARLIC

SIDE FOR 4

These jaunty parcels are a nice showcase for mushrooms; their earthy richness pairs beautifully with the dates and walnuts. Baking everything together in a sealed packet allows the mushrooms to cook gently, without browning, and to absorb the flavors of the rest of the ingredients. It also means you get to unwrap part of your meal at the table like a delicious little gift.

If you're lucky enough to come across desert truffles (see The Hot Date! Pantry, page 38), you can use them here: Peel, slice, and boil in milk before adding them to your fungi party.

2 lbs [910 g] assorted fresh mushrooms, cleaned and chopped into bite-size pieces

1 to 2 dried porcini mushrooms, crumbled into pieces about the size of a pencil eraser

3 garlic cloves, grated with a Microplane or very finely minced

3 thyme sprigs and/or other herbs of your choice, such as chives, parsley, or oregano

3 Tbsp roughly chopped raw walnuts

3 large or 5 small dates, pitted and roughly chopped

¼ cup [60 ml] olive or walnut oil

1 tsp salt

½ tsp freshly ground black pepper

1 tsp fresh lemon juice

3 Tbsp butter, cut into small cubes

Fresh herbs, such as parsley, to garnish

Preheat the oven to 400°F [200°C]. Lay a few large squares of parchment paper on top of each other on a rimmed baking sheet.

In a medium bowl, toss together the fresh and dried mushrooms, garlic, thyme, walnuts, dates, and olive or walnut oil. Add the salt and pepper, squeeze over the lemon juice, then spoon into the center of the parchment. Dot the top of this mixture with little cubes of butter. Tie the parcel up with kitchen twine, pulling the four corners up to meet each other and knotting below. Bake for 25 minutes, or until the package puffs up with steam and the mushrooms are fully cooked. Carefully transfer the entire packet to a serving platter and immediately unfurl at the table (watch out for steam!). Sprinkle with parsley, and serve.

CARAMELIZED OKRA

SIDE FOR 4

Blistered, burnished okra—a little sweet, a little savory: This dish is a celebration of the very specific flavor and texture that make this vegetable so special. I cook this year-round using frozen packages of teeny tiny "okra zero," which are no bigger than the tip of your finger and widely available at Middle Eastern grocery stores. If you can't find okra zero or are using fresh okra, trim the tops off the okra and slice into ½ inch [13 mm] thick coins. Looking to luxe things up a little? Serve with butter-toasted pine nuts, spooned over just before serving, or add slabs of Halloumi cheese to the skillet just before the final broil.

Serve the okra with rice or other ballast to make this a meal—we often eat it alongside orzo loaded up with miso butter, kalamata olives, and grape tomatoes.

2 Tbsp date molasses, plus more for serving

Juice of ½ lemon, plus more for serving

½ tsp chili paste of your choice (harissa, sambal oelek, yuzu kosho . . .)

1 tsp salt

2 Tbsp olive oil, plus more for serving

4 garlic cloves, thinly sliced

14 oz [400 g] okra, trimmed if needed

Big pinch of torn fresh mint (about 2 Tbsp)

1 fresh red chile, thinly sliced (optional)

Heat the broiler to high.

In a small bowl, combine the date molasses, lemon juice, chili paste, salt, and ¼ cup [60 ml] of water. Mix thoroughly and set aside.

In an ovenproof skillet or sauté pan over medium heat, warm the olive oil, then add the garlic and cook until fragrant and just starting to turn golden, about 1 minute. Add the date molasses mixture and bring to a boil, then add the okra, cover, and cook over medium heat for 5 minutes. (If you're using frozen okra, you do not need to thaw it beforehand.) Remove the lid and cook until the liquid is reduced and coats the okra in a thick, shiny mantle, about 5 more minutes. Watch out—it burns easily.

Slide the pan under the broiler and broil for about 5 minutes. The okra should take on lots of color at this point, charring, blistering, and caramelizing in the heat.

Serve sprinkled with torn mint and sliced red chile, along with a further squeeze of lemon and a drizzle each of the date molasses and olive oil.

SHIPWRECKED & BEDECKED in PALM FRONDS to PRESERVE HIS MODESTY, ODYSSEUS
ENCOUNTERS NAUSICAA on the BEACH i this EXCERPT from THE ODYSSEY.

MALE FLOWER

FEMALE FLOWER

INFLORESCENCE
of MALE FLOWERS

FEMALE SPADIX in FLOWER

DATE
BLOSSOMS
POLLINATED
& BAGGED

TH
FE
LEF
A GRO
the
SINGLE MA
THEY WALK
IN ITS OWN LIT
FILTERING THROUG
EARLY ENOUGH IN T
IN the LATE AFTER
SPATHE TO PLAY WIT
TO CLENCH IN H
EAT THEM — HE IS
VERY EXCITED, THE
AGREE ON WHAT, PR

A VISIT to A DATE FARM

in AL AWIR, DUBAI

EVERY SPRING, the FARM OWNERS—BELOVED
[FA]MILY FRIENDS—SEND MY PARENTS SPRIGS of
[MA]LE DATE BLOSSOMS to POLLINATE THEIR TREES.
[TH]E FLOWERS ARE PLUNGED INTO the EMERGING
[FEMAL]E BLOSSOMS & PROTECTED WITH BROWN PAPER BAGS,
[to] PLAY THEIR ROLE. WHEN WE VISIT, WE'RE MET BY
[the] FRIENDLY FARMERS WHO ARE HAPPY TO EXPLAIN
[the ES]OTERIC MYSTERIES of DATE PROPAGATION. A
[male PA]LM CAN POLLINATE UP TO 50 FEMALE PALMS!
[WE PAS]S THROUGH AVENUES of SHADY TREES, EACH
[in its] DIVOT of SANDY EARTH. THE SUN
[on the] SPIKY LEAVES IS STRONG, THOUGH IT IS STILL
[early in the] YEAR THAT WE ARE COMFORTABLE OUTDOORS
[at no]ON. THE FARMHANDS GIVE QAIS A DATE
[and the]N A POSY OF DATE BLOSSOMS FOR HIM
[to cl]UMP, LITTLE FIST. WHEN HE STARTS TO
[...] MONTHS OLD, AFTER ALL—EVERYONE GETS
[...S]YMBOLIZE SOMETHING GOOD, THOUGH NO ONE CAN
[...SURE]LY: WISDOM, POWER, GOOD JUDGEMENT, FERTILITY...

SWEETS

CHAPTER 5

PEANUT BUTTER— STUFFED CHOCOLATE— COVERED DATES

12 PIECES, MULTIPLIES EASILY

Every time I go back to Dubai to visit my parents, I make sure to stock up on a giant bag of chocolate-covered dates at the airport duty free on my way back to Brooklyn. There's something about the sweet, chewy date encased in a chocolate shell that is irresistible. The commercial kind are usually stuffed with a variety of nuts, but you can serve them plain or with more unusual fillings if you're feeling a tad experimental. Peanut butter is always a crowd-pleaser. Take a look at the suggestions for stuffed dates on page 254 if you're looking for further inspiration.

12 large dates, such as jumbo Medjools, pitted

6 Tbsp peanut butter, creamy or chunky (optional)

6 oz [170 g] dark chocolate

Line a baking sheet with parchment paper and set aside.

If you are stuffing the dates, do so now. Use about a teaspoon of peanut butter each—it will depend on the size of your date. Close the date completely over the filling, so that none is peeking out, and try not to smear any on the outside of the date.

Using a food processor or a sharp chef's knife, chop the chocolate into very small pieces. Set aside one quarter of the chocolate. Melt the remaining three quarters of the chocolate using either a microwave or a double boiler. If using a microwave, melt in a medium glass bowl for 20 seconds at a time, stirring in between, until the chocolate is smooth and shiny. If using a double boiler, place the chocolate in the top and melt, stirring continuously. Be sure not to let the bottom of the boiler touch the hot water. Once the chocolate is melted, add the remaining quarter of the chocolate and stir until completely smooth. If you have one, a candy thermometer is helpful here: The chocolate should reach 88°F [30°C].

Using two forks or a pair of chopsticks, dip the dates one at a time into the melted chocolate, then leave to set on the parchment-lined baking sheet. You may need to refrigerate for a couple of minutes to get the chocolate to firm up. Serve right away. The dates will keep, tightly covered in the refrigerator, for up to a week.

DATE DIBS ICE CREAM

ABOUT 1½ PT [700 G] ICE CREAM

This is the richest, easiest ice cream base you will ever make—all you need is milk, cream, and dibs (date molasses) and you are most of the way to an ice cream that remains soft and scoopable even after a long stint in the freezer. The combination of lemon zest and cinnamon is subtle but hauntingly delicious, particularly if you treat yourself to an affogato by drowning a scoop in a shot of espresso—the richness of the date ice cream plays wonderfully against hot, bitter coffee.

For a fresher variation, omit the lemon and cinnamon and steep two big handfuls of fresh mint in the mixture overnight. Strain out the mint in the morning and continue as written.

Mix-ins: Layer torn rutab dates into the freshly churned ice cream for a caramel ripple effect, or crumble in chunks of Dibs Hokey Pokey (page 216) for a killer honeycomb candy ice cream.

2 cups [475 ml] heavy cream

1 cup [240 ml] whole milk

½ cup [120 ml] date molasses

¼ tsp ground cinnamon

¼ tsp salt

4 strips lemon peel, peeled using a vegetable peeler and each about ½ in [1 cm] wide

In a medium saucepan, combine the heavy cream, milk, date molasses, cinnamon, and salt and stir gently to dissolve the date molasses. Set the mixture over medium-low heat, stirring occasionally, and pull from the heat as soon as tiny bubbles start to form around the edge of the pan, 3 to 4 minutes. Try to heat this mixture as gently as possible; if it comes to a boil the date molasses may curdle the dairy, which will affect the texture of the ice cream. Once the tiny bubbles form, the mixture will have visibly thickened. This is good.

Add the strips of lemon, cover, and steep at room temperature for 1 hour. Refrigerate until it is completely chilled, at least 2 hours and preferably overnight.

Remove the strips of lemon peel from the mixture and give it a good brisk stir. I like to use an immersion blender to ensure the smoothest texture, but it is not necessary. Transfer to an ice cream maker and freeze according to the manufacturer's instructions. The ice cream is ready when it is the texture of soft serve. Enjoy right away or freeze in an airtight container for up to 3 weeks—the ice cream won't retain its soft serve texture, but it will still be easy to scoop.

CHOCOLATE SORBET WITH WARM SALTED DATES

ABOUT 2 PT [940 G]

A very rich, very intense delivery mechanism for dark chocolate, this sorbet cuts out anything that might distract from the chocolate itself, omitting the muffling effect of eggs and cream and keeping the focus squarely on the cacao. Use the best cocoa powder and chocolate you can get your hands on, as there isn't anything for the chocolate to hide behind. I love to serve little scoops of this at the end of a rich meal, along with a similarly sized cup of espresso or Turkish coffee for each guest.

As with the other very chocolate-forward recipes in this chapter, dates are the backup dancers to chocolate's Beyoncé: Think of the date molasses as a flavor enhancer, not the star of the show. That said, if you are making this in early autumn, when rutab dates are in season, try folding them directly into the just-churned ice cream for a luscious ready-to-go date ripple. I also highly recommend serving this with the optional Warm Salted Dates (recipe follows), which act like a sort of super-charged hot fudge—try tumbling a few chewy dates in their oil over a scoop of sorbet and thank me later.

If you don't have an ice cream maker (or, uh, forgot to freeze the cylinder in time), don't worry: This also makes a luscious chocolate pudding. Pour it into little cups, like shot glasses or tea cups, and let set overnight in the refrigerator. Top with crème fraîche and a little cracked cardamom, and serve with your tiniest spoons.

Last, but not least, this sorbet is also mind-blowing as part of an ice cream sundae: Top with warmed dates, slightly overwhipped cream, salted and deeply toasted chopped almonds, and, of course, a cherry on top.

¾ cup [60 g] unsweetened cocoa powder

½ cup [100 g] sugar

½ cup [120 ml] date molasses

¼ tsp salt

8 oz [225 g] bittersweet chocolate, finely chopped

½ tsp instant coffee powder (optional)

½ tsp vanilla extract (optional)

Big pinch of flaky salt

In a large pot set over medium-high heat, whisk 1½ cups [360 ml] of water with the cocoa powder, sugar, date molasses, and salt. Bring to a boil, whisking frequently, then continue whisking for 1 minute more. Remove from the heat, and stir in the chopped chocolate. Let stand, undisturbed, for a full minute, then stir in the instant coffee powder (if using), vanilla (if using), and 1 cup [240 ml] of water. Use an immersion blender to blend the mixture in the pot until silky smooth. If you don't have an immersion blender, you can use a regular blender or a hand whisk. Chill the mixture in the refrigerator until it is completely cold, at least 3 hours and preferably overnight.

Just before you churn the ice cream, give it another good whisk to get it aerated and fluid again—I like to use an immersion blender at this point to ensure the smoothest texture, but it isn't a necessary step. Transfer the mixture to an ice cream maker and freeze according to the machine's instructions. Serve plain, with a spoonful of whipped cream or crème fraîche, or with the warm salted dates that follow. Either way, do not skimp on the flaky salt as a final finish.

CONT'D

WARM SALTED DATES

DATES FOR 1, MULTIPLIES EASILY

Use soft and yielding dates: juicy Med-jools, not hard Sukkaris or Deglet Nours.

2 dates per serving

½ Tbsp per serving good olive, pumpkin seed, pecan, or walnut oil

Flaky salt

Halve and pit each date, then heat up a skillet and drizzle in half a tablespoon of oil per serving. When the oil is just warm, place the dates, cut-side down, in the skillet and gently heat them just enough to warm the dates and coax out the flavor of the oil, not kill it. Remove from the heat and sprinkle with a delicate large-flake salt, such as Maldon. Top each serving of ice cream with the still-warm dates and then drizzle over the flavored oil, adding more salt if needed.

HOT DATE! HOT FUDGE

ABOUT 1½ CUPS [360 ML]

Glossy glossy glossy, thick, and almost chewy. A slow-moving lava flow hardening against cold ice cream, this hot fudge is pure summertime bliss, but it can also be a year-round treat. It's good with plain yogurt! Slathered on strawberries! Eaten out of the jar with a spoon! Spread on toast! And, of course, fulfilling its highest calling: as the topping on a banana split (see page 184).

Note that the date molasses is not super identifiable here, but it makes for an unrivaled more-chocolate-than-chocolate, deep-dark-delightful situation. Use a chocolate you'd enjoy eating on its own, and avoid chocolate chips, as they have stabilizers in them that can cause mild chaos when it comes to melting and reheating.

A wee (literally) serving suggestion: Tiny date sundaes. Pit some dates, preferably jumbo Medjools, and fill each one with a spoonful of vanilla ice cream, then drizzle with hot fudge and a cheery spritz of whipped cream. Do not neglect the cherry on top. You can prep these ahead, as the freezer-friendly fudge won't fully harden in the cold.

1 cup [240 ml] heavy cream
½ cup [120 ml] date molasses
¼ cup [50 g] sugar
2 Tbsp salted butter
¼ tsp salt
2 oz [55 g] semisweet chocolate, cut or smashed into small pieces
¾ cup [60 g] unsweetened cocoa powder, sifted if lumpy

In a small saucepan over medium-low heat, combine the heavy cream, date molasses, sugar, butter, and salt and stir until simmering. Let simmer for 1 minute, then add the semisweet chocolate and cocoa powder and whisk continuously until very glossy and gently blurping and oozing. Continue whisking for another 3 minutes. Whisk diligently! If it's still lumpy, give it a whizz with an immersion blender until smooth, thick, and slightly chewy. Remove from the heat and let cool slightly, then transfer to a heatproof container and let stand. The flavors will meld and deepen as the fudge sits—at least 1 hour is advisable, though not essential. Rewarm the fudge very gently in a saucepan over low heat; it burns easily. (You can also warm it in short bursts in the microwave or use a bain-marie/double boiler.) The fudge will keep, covered in the refrigerator, for up to 1 week. Serve warm, in generous dollops over scoops of your favorite ice cream.

ANATOMY of ~ BANANA SPLIT

1 · DATE DIBS ICE CREAM · 2 · CHOCOLATE SORBET · 3 · DIBS HOKEY POKEY ·
4 · HOT DATE! HOT FUDGE · 5 · WALNUTS in DATE HONEY ·
6 · RAS el HANOUT DATE SYRUP · 7 · BURNT DATE HONEY ·
8 · WARM SALTED DATES · 9 · HALWA CRUMBLES ·
10 · POMEGRANATE SEED SPRINKLES · 11 · ROSE PETALS · 12 · PISTACHIO POWDER
13 · WHIPPED CREAM · 14 · LA BANANE · 15 · the CHERRY on TOP!

SILKY CHOCOLATE-DATE TRUFFLES

ABOUT 30 TRUFFLES

"Silky" for the combination of luscious rutab against the mousse-like chocolate, the seam of plump jeweled dates running through the block of ganache like a vein of precious ore in a mine. Pop one of these truffles whole into your mouth and let it melt slowly on your tongue . . . transcendent. You can make this recipe without using rutab-stage dates, or indeed without dates at all—it's always good to have a signature truffle recipe in your back pocket—but the right dates are worth waiting for, because they melt into the texture of the chocolate and add a plush, elusive richness. If you handed a truffle to someone without explaining they had dates in them, they might not be able to guess the secret ingredient at all.

If it is not already clear, this is not the place to use so-so chocolate; you want at least 60% and for it to be a chocolate you'd be happy to eat on its own. Avoid stabilizer-laden chocolate chips, as they will affect the set of the truffles. The date syrup is optional, but helps to maintain the silky texture of the truffle.

9 oz [255 g] 60 or 65 percent dark chocolate

¾ cup [180 ml] heavy or whipping cream

1 Tbsp butter

1 Tbsp date syrup (optional)

Big pinch of flaky salt

6 to 10 soft, yielding dates, ideally at the rutab stage of ripeness

2 Tbsp cocoa powder, sifted if lumpy

Line a small, deep baking pan with parchment paper, leaving about 1 in [2.5 cm] hanging over the sides. I use a 6 in [15 cm] square baking pan, which makes for deep cubes once the truffles are sliced. You can use a larger pan, but your truffles will be thinner.

Finely chop the chocolate. The smaller the pieces, the more evenly they will melt. If you are in a certain sort of mood, you can also very satisfyingly smash the chocolate, still in its wrapper, against a countertop or other hard surface. Aim for smithereens.

In a small saucepan over medium heat, warm the heavy cream and the butter until almost boiling. Look for tiny bubbles forming just at the edges of the pan. The butter should melt fully as you gently swirl the mixture around. Remove the pan from the heat, then add the chopped chocolate and let stand, undisturbed, for 2 minutes, so the residual heat from the cream melts the chocolate. Add the date syrup (if using) and salt and whisk until smooth and glossy with no lumps. If you have an immersion blender, using it to whip the cream and chocolate will create a more stable emulsion. If you don't have one, don't worry—just whisk with verve and commitment until the mixture is shiny and smooth.

Pour half of the mixture into the prepared pan, then dot with the torn date halves. Pour the remaining chocolate over the dates to cover completely. Rap the bottom of the pan against your countertop a couple of times to dislodge any air bubbles and ensure the ganache is evenly spread. Keep the surface as smooth as possible. Freeze the mixture for 2 to 3 hours to firm up the chocolate.

Remove the pan from the freezer and use the parchment to lift the chocolate mixture from the pan. Use a sharp knife to cut the chocolate into 1 in [2.5 cm] cubes, wiping down your knife between cuts if needed to keep the slices clean.

Put the cocoa powder into a shallow bowl. Using a fork or offset spatula, drop one truffle cube at a time into the cocoa and gently toss to coat on all sides. Tap off any excess cocoa powder, then place each truffle on a serving tray. The truffles will keep, in an airtight container in the refrigerator, for 1 to 2 weeks; enjoy cold or at room temperature.

WHOLE ROASTED PINEAPPLE DRAPED IN SPICED CARAMEL

DESSERT FOR 6

A ludicrous little creature that cuts a fine figure at any dinner table, there is something irresistibly anthropomorphic about this pineapple, bristling with vanilla bean spears and defying anyone who approaches it not to find it charming (and slightly terrifying). I wish I could claim the credit for the vanilla beans myself, but I learned this trick from a recipe by New York City–based spice purveyors La Boîte. As the vanilla-pierced pineapple roasts in the oven, it gives off puffs of deliciously scented air and preens with every application of its lacquered cloak. When it emerges, slightly heat-slumped and tender to its heart, it is ready to take its place as the star of the dinner table.

There are a few tips for testing grocery-store pineapples for ripeness. You should be able to easily pull a leaf out of the central crown; the exterior of the pineapple should be yellow-brown, not green; and the fruit should be notably fragrant, particularly if you turn it upside down and take a sniff.

The plumper and fresher your vanilla bean, the easier it will be to slice it into spears. If your bean is too old, it might break into smaller shards. Don't worry if this happens: Stick the largest pieces into the pineapple and chuck the remainder into the base of the pan;

they'll flavor the spiced syrup and won't go to waste.

1 ripe pineapple

¼ cup [60 ml] date molasses

Zest and juice of 1 lime

1 tsp five-spice powder

½ tsp mild red chili flakes, such as Aleppo or Urfa biber

1 vanilla bean

Preheat the oven to 350°F [180°C].

Using a sharp knife or vegetable peeler, peel the pineapple. Use a large, sharp knife to cut off the bottom of the pineapple so it stands flat, then place it upright in a deep roasting pan.

In a small bowl, whisk together the date molasses, lime zest and juice, five-spice powder, and red chili flakes. Spoon or brush the mixture over the entire pineapple until thickly coated. You should have some syrup left, which you will use to baste the pineapple as it roasts.

With a small sharp knife, carefully cut the vanilla bean lengthwise in half. Cut each length into thirds to make six long, thin pieces in total. Use your knife to make six deep incisions around the perimeter of the pineapple, then carefully slide a length of vanilla bean into each.

Your pineapple should look slightly sentient and devil-may-care, like a rogue Dalek or a cheerful little horned demon. If any vanilla bean seeds linger on your fingertips, rub them along your pulse points—your wrists, the base of your neck, behind your ears—and revel in the beautiful scent.

Roast the pineapple, basting it often with the spiced syrup, until the fruit is soft and tender and the caramelized exterior is bubbling. You should be able to slide a knife into the heart of the pineapple with little to no resistance. This can take anywhere from 45 to 90 minutes.

Bring the pineapple to the table amid much fanfare, and carve it in front of your guests. Serve sliced, like a cake, with the remaining juices passed alongside, or supplement with vanilla ice cream or lightly sweetened crème fraîche. This dessert is best the day it is made, but the roasted pineapple will keep up to 2 days, refrigerated. Gently warm leftovers.

SUMMER PLUMS IN DATE SYRUP

DESSERT FOR 6

Poached fruit is the perfect celebration of summer, partially because it's a distillation of the purest essence of the fruit itself, but mostly because you don't have to turn the oven on during the hottest of days. This two-ingredient recipe tastes far more complex than the sum of its parts, for very little effort. Pile ripe plums—or apricots or pluots or nectarines, whatever stone fruit looks best at the market—into a juicy mountain, drizzle generously with date molasses, and cook. You don't even need to add water, as you are going to very gently poach the fruit in its own juices, alongside the honeyed influence of the date molasses. The plums infuse the syrup with flavor and turn it the most beautiful elusive red-brown.

Serve with some lush dairy (crème fraîche, mascarpone, whipped cream, vanilla ice cream . . .) and a sprinkling of crushed pistachios or pine nuts, or tumble some plums into your morning granola and yogurt for a very special breakfast. The syrup makes a wonderful cocktail mixer and is a treat with plain seltzer water and much crushed ice. I've given rough amounts here, but it is a very forgiving combination and almost any ratio of ripe fruit to syrup will yield good results.

2½ lbs [1.1 kg] small ripe plums
1½ cups [360 ml] date molasses

Pile the plums into a small, deep pan—you want to make a mound of them, not spread them out. Pour over the date molasses and set the pan over medium heat. Stir gently until you see the plums getting juicy, then simmer for 20 to 30 minutes, occasionally nudging the plums that are on the bottom to make room for the ones on top. The plums are done when their flesh is yielding and easily pierced to the stone with a knife; they should have emitted copious amounts of honeyed juices, with skin that is peeling and flaking off the flesh. You can serve these warm or chilled; I peel and pit them if I want a slightly more refined-looking dessert, but as often as not leave them be, raggedy and delicious. Stored in an airtight container, the plums will keep in the refrigerator for up to 10 days.

SUMMER GOLD FRUIT SALAD

FRUIT SALAD FOR 4

A monochrome late-summer delight, its glinting gold like the gleaming coins of a dragon's hoard. Make this during the magic window when the last of summer's stone fruit intersects with the first khalal-stage dates, crispy and crunchy like sugar apples. Look for stone fruit in sunset colors on the yellow spectrum: plums, peaches, nectarines, apricots, and pluots, the more vibrant the better.

This salad is best left to marinate a few hours, even overnight, so that the flavors have time to marry and the dried apricots completely rehydrate. The dates will retain their crunch, even a couple of days later, so it's a great make-ahead dish.

10 to 12 golden Barhi or other khalal-stage dates, pitted and cut into thin crescents

¼ cup [30 g] dried apricots, scissored into thin strips

1 lb [450 g] juicy yellow fresh stone fruit, pitted and cut into spoonable pieces

2 Tbsp fresh lime juice

1 Tbsp date molasses, maple syrup, or honey

¼ tsp ground ginger

Olive oil, torn fresh mint, flaky salt, for serving

In a large bowl, combine the dates, dried apricots, fresh stone fruit, lime juice, date molasses, and ground ginger. Stir to mix thoroughly. Leave to chill in the refrigerator for at least 2 hours. Serve drizzled with the thinnest thread of olive oil and sprinkled with mint and just enough salt to make the flavors pop. The fruit salad is lovely on its own or bolstered by ice cream, whipped cream, or the fiery crunch of ginger biscuits or Spice Route Molasses Cookies (page 193).

SPICE ROUTE MOLASSES COOKIES

2 TO 3 DOZEN LITTLE COOKIES

Named for the ancient maritime spice trade that brought these flavors to the rest of the world, these tiny, intense cookies are like gingersnaps with more zing to them. Think of them as the baked goods edition of the Winter Elixir (page 235), each cookie a chewy, bracing little bite that unfurls into a burst of warm spices in your mouth, with a deep, dark note of date molasses thrumming underneath. They're lovely paired with a cup of coffee or a bite of date; I often bake a batch when I'm spinning up some Date Dibs Ice Cream (page 179) and make teeny ice cream sandwiches to serve after dinner.

½ cup [113 g] butter, at room temperature

⅔ cup [130 g] sugar

Zest of 1 lemon

1½ cups [210 g] flour

3 Tbsp ground ginger

1 Tbsp ground turmeric

½ Tbsp ground cinnamon

½ tsp freshly ground black pepper

¾ Tbsp baking soda

1¼ tsp baking powder

½ tsp salt

½ cup plus 1 Tbsp [135 ml] date molasses

½ cup [100 g] turbinado sugar, for rolling

Preheat the oven to 350°F [180°C]. Line two baking sheets with parchment paper.

In the bowl of a mixer fitted with the paddle, cream the butter and sugar with the lemon zest until pale and fluffy. In another large bowl, sift together the flour, ginger, turmeric, cinnamon, and pepper, along with the baking soda and baking powder, then stir in the salt. Add the flour mixture to the butter mixture and stir just enough to bring it together; it should still be crumbly. Add the date molasses and mix gently, just until the dough pulls together.

Put the turbinado sugar in a small shallow bowl. Roll tiny balls of the dough, the size of large marbles, between your palms. You can use a tablespoon as a dough scoop. Roll the dough balls, one at a time, in the turbinado sugar to completely coat, then set them on the prepared baking sheets, leaving a couple of inches of clearance between them. Bake for 10 to 12 minutes, or until the tops of the cookies are set and the bottoms are uniformly golden. Let cool at least 10 minutes before serving. The cookies will keep for up to 2 weeks, with the spice flavor intensifying over time. You can also freeze the unbaked cookie dough after you've rolled it in the sugar; just bake it for a little longer if you do.

SALTED HALWA BROWNIE COOKIES

12 TO 15 COOKIES

A salty, chocolaty joy-storm, with clouds of halwa and little lightning bolts of chewy date sprinkled throughout. Make these for someone you love (who loves chocolate).

4 Tbsp [55 g] butter

7 oz [200 g] 70% dark chocolate, cut into small pieces

⅔ cup [70 g] flour

3 Tbsp unsweetened cocoa powder, sifted if lumpy

1 tsp baking powder

½ tsp salt

2 eggs, at room temperature

½ cup [100 g] granulated sugar

½ cup [100 g] date sugar or packed light brown sugar

1 tsp vanilla extract

7 to 10 dates (about 3.5 oz [100 g]), pitted and roughly chopped

5 oz [140 g] halwa, cut into ½ in [13 mm] cubes

½ cup [85 g] semisweet chocolate chips

Flaky salt, like Maldon or fleur de sel, for sprinkling

Preheat the oven to 350°F [180°C]. Line two baking sheets with parchment paper.

In a small saucepan over low heat, melt the butter. Add the chocolate and let it sit in its butter bath for about 60 seconds, then stir until completely smooth.

In a large bowl, sift together the flour, 2 tablespoons of the cocoa powder, the baking powder, and the salt.

In another large bowl, whisk together the eggs, granulated sugar, date sugar, and vanilla until light and frothy, about 5 minutes. Whisk in the melted chocolate mixture. Add this eggy chocolate mixture to the flour mixture and fold until just combined.

Toss the chopped dates with the remaining 1 tablespoon of cocoa powder, then fold into the cookie dough along with the halwa and chocolate chips. The dough will look more like brownie batter than your average cookie dough, but it should still hold its shape on the baking sheet. Using an ice cream scoop or a pair of spoons, scoop the dough onto the prepared baking sheets, leaving about 3 in [7.5 cm] between each cookie.

Bake for 12 to 14 minutes, or until the tops are crackled and shiny. Sprinkle the cookies with flaky salt and let cool before serving. The cookies will keep in an airtight container for up to 4 days.

ANCIENT EGYPTIAN TIGER-NUT CAKES
from the TOMB of REKHMIRE

CONE-SHAPED CAKELETS FAVORED BY the PHAROAH — A "RECIPE" THAT CAN BE READ in the PICTOGRAMS on the WALLS of AN EGYPTIAN NOBLE'S TOMB.

TIGER NUTS ARE GUMMY LITTLE TUBERS WITH A MILD, NUTTY FLAVOR.

POUND TIGER NUTS INTO FLOUR, THEN COMBINE WITH HONEY, OIL and DATES. STIR MIXTURE OVER LOW HEAT, THEN COOL and SHAPE INTO LONG CONES. STACK the CAKES IN BASKETS and OFFER AS SACRIFICES to the SUN GOD AMUN.

BLACK TAHINI CHOCOLATE CHIP COOKIES

20 TO 25 COOKIES

These chocolate chip cookies are a great showcase for different types of dates. I like to tear up multiple varieties as a way to get a sampling—widely available Medjools work well, but consider chewy Sukkaris, raisiny Ajwas, and caramelly Khalas. The cookies' crisp exteriors and fudgy interiors are the perfect platform for bitter chocolate, rich sesame, sweet date, and crunchy salt. The tahini makes these a particularly appealing cookie for fans of the chocolate and peanut butter vibe.

The melted butter makes for fudgier cookies with dense centers, as opposed to the more common creamed room temperature butter and sugar approach. Because you're using melted butter, the dough needs to rest for at least 8 hours in the refrigerator, preferably overnight or longer.

I like to use chocolate fèves or wafers, which come in bigger, more satisfying chunks, but you can use regular chocolate chips here too. The soy sauce may seem a little left field, but it adds very necessary umami undertones, and it works totally in the background. You won't taste it, but it amps up the other flavors.

A couple of tahini tips: Be sure your tahini is well stirred and any oil is completely incorporated before you use it. I tested these multiple times, with both regular tahini and Chinese roasted black sesame paste. The cookies are delicious with plain old tahini, but if you can get your hands on black sesame paste, please do try it here! It's much more rich and robust, slightly bitter and earthy—a worthy foil to the sweet dates.

½ cup [113 g] butter, melted

1 cup [200 g] sugar

½ cup [130 g] black sesame paste or tahini

2 eggs, at room temperature

2 tsp soy sauce

1¼ cups [175 g] flour

½ tsp baking powder

½ tsp baking soda

½ tsp salt

8 to 12 dates, pitted and torn into irregular quarters

1½ cups [240 g] chocolate chips, wafers, or fêves

Flaky salt, for sprinkling

In a large bowl, whisk together the melted butter and sugar until combined. Make sure the sesame paste doesn't have any lumps or separated oil, then add to the butter mixture and whisk to incorporate. Whisk in the eggs, one at a time, until they are completely incorporated and the mixture is visibly paler. Stir in the soy sauce.

In a medium bowl, sift together the flour, baking powder, and baking soda. Stir in the salt. Add the flour mixture to the egg mixture and fold until just combined. Don't overwork the dough. Fold in the dates and chocolate, then cover and leave to rest in the refrigerator for at least 8 hours and preferably at least 24 hours.

Preheat the oven to 325°F [165°C].

Use an ice cream scoop to shape the dough into golf ball–sized pieces and set them about 3 in [7.5 cm] apart on a baking sheet. Sprinkle the cookies with flaky salt. Bake for 12 to 17 minutes, or until golden brown at the edges and set on top. Leave to cool, then eat.

If you use black sesame paste, it will be difficult to detect any visible browning, since the dough is already so dark. Pull the cookies closer to the 12-minute mark; when baked, the glossy black cookie dough will be paler and matte charcoal gray, with some browning at the edges, and the cookies will look just set on top and at the edges.

This cookie dough freezes well. Portion it out with an ice cream scoop and freeze, uncovered, on a baking sheet, then transfer to a freezer-safe container. The frozen dough will keep for several months, and the cookies can be baked, one at a time, whenever the mood strikes you.

HOT MIX CHOCOLATE CHIP COOKIES

15 TO 20 COOKIES

This is a one-bowl chocolate chip cookie that grabs you by the lapels and insists upon your full attention. There's just so much going on: The explosive pops of flavor and texture provided by the mix-ins sing in contrast to the rich, bitter chocolate. An infusion of date sugar keeps the cookie dough soft and chewy, adding a background caramel flavor that is the perfect canvas for the aforementioned fireworks.

Hot mix, Bombay mix, namkeen, chevdo, chewra—if you have not already enjoyed the bounty of Indian snack mixes, you are missing out. Imagine a flurry of fried nodules and twists fallen from clouds of dream-level spices, dotted with juicy dried fruit and crunchy nuts. Then tack on a few more flourishes: fried curry leaves! spiced cornflakes! crunchy lentils! Recipes vary by family and by region, but they are all delicious. You can find pre-made versions online or in Indian/South Asian grocery stores. My personal favorite for the following recipe is Haldiram's Cornflakes Mixture, but any mixes that use a variety of ingredients will do; look for types with names such as Khatta Meetha, All-in-One, Kashmiri Mixture, Chewda, Bombay Mix, or Shahi Mix. Really, you can't go wrong.

This recipe also calls for pearl sugar, which is the type of sugar used to make Belgian-style waffles. Pearl sugar doesn't dissolve during baking, so it adds another layer of texture and crunch to the cookies. It's particularly delicious if you are using a snack mix that leans savory, less relevant if yours is already quite sweet. If you can't find pearl sugar, you can omit it from the recipe—just throw in a few raisins or chopped dates to bring the cookies more firmly into salty-sweet territory, or add a couple of additional tablespoons of regular sugar to the dough base.

Note that these cookies are best baked soon after you mix the dough; the date sugar continues to hydrate and can dry out the cookies if left too long unbaked.

½ cup [113 g] butter, melted

½ cup [100 g] sugar

½ cup [65 g] date sugar

1 tsp kosher salt

½ tsp baking powder

½ tsp baking soda

1 large egg

1 tsp vanilla extract

1⅓ cups [185 g] flour

¼ cup [50 g] pearl sugar (optional)

1 cup [160 g] chocolate chips, wafers, or fêves

2 cups [around 225 g] Indian snack mix of your choice

Preheat the oven to 375°F [190°C]. Line two baking sheets with parchment paper.

In a large bowl, add the butter, sugar, date sugar, salt, baking powder, and baking soda. Stir until blended. Add the egg and the vanilla and stir until smooth. Set the mixture aside for 15 to 20 minutes so the date sugar can hydrate.

Add the flour and stir just until a soft, smooth dough forms. Stir in the pearl sugar (if using), chocolate chips, and the snack mix until just combined. Use an ice cream scoop to shape the dough into ping pong ball-sized pieces and set them about 1 inch [2.5 cm] apart on the prepared baking sheets.

Bake, one tray at a time, on the center oven rack until golden around the edges, 10 to 13 minutes. Keep a close watch as they bake; the date sugar makes them particularly prone to burning on the bottom. The baked cookies will still be soft, and will firm up as they cool. Transfer immediately to a wire rack to cool. Store in an airtight container for up to 4 days.

HOW
FAIR
and HOW
PLEASANT
ART THOU, O LOVE,
FOR DELIGHTS!
THIS THY STATURE IS LIKE
TO A PALM TREE, and
THY BREASTS TO
CLUSTERS of GRAPES.
I SAID, I WILL GO UP TO
the PALM TREE,
I WILL TAKE HOLD of the
BOUGHS THEREOF.

- from
THE
SONG of
SOLOMON
(7:6-8)

LIME & GINGER CRUNCH

ABOUT 20 SHORTBREAD FINGERS

Spicy, crumbly, crunchy, buttery—these cookies feature a melt-in-your-mouth shortbread base that's topped with a thick and toothsome layer of date syrup and ginger "caramel" icing, and studded with gem-like chunks of date, chopped ginger, and slivered pistachio. The recipe is a riff on ginger crunch, a beloved New Zealand teatime treat that I became obsessed with the moment I saw its spectacular icing-to-shortbread ratio. Speaking of: Be sure to pour the icing over the shortbread base while it's still warm from the oven so it sets up right.

SHORTBREAD

Zest of 1 lime

½ cup [100 g] granulated sugar

9 Tbsp [135 g] butter, at room temperature

1½ cups [180 g] flour

2 tsp ground ginger

1 tsp baking powder

½ tsp salt

"CARAMEL" ICING

10 Tbsp [150 g] butter

¼ cup [60 ml] date molasses

1½ cups [180 g] confectioners' sugar

4 tsp ground ginger

Pinch of salt

½ cup [90 g] crystallized ginger, cut into bite-size pieces

½ cup [75 g] pitted dates, cut into bite-size pieces

¼ cup [30 g] slivered pistachios (optional)

TO MAKE THE SHORTBREAD, preheat the oven to 350°F [180°C]. Butter an 8 in [20 cm] square baking pan, then line it with parchment paper.

In the bowl of a mixer fitted with the paddle, use your fingers to rub the lime zest into the granulated sugar to release the citrus oils. Add the butter and beat until pale and fluffy.

In a medium bowl, sift together the flour, ground ginger, baking powder, and salt. Add to the butter mixture and fold gently to combine. It will be dry and crumbly. Gently knead the dough just until it comes together (overworking it will make the shortbread tough), then press it into the prepared pan, using the pads of your fingers to press it evenly all the way to the edges. Use an offset spatula or the back of a spoon to smooth the top. Bake for 20 to 25 minutes, or until the shortbread is pale gold and slightly darker at the edges. It will still be a little soft to the touch when you take it out of the oven but will harden as it cools.

Meanwhile, **TO MAKE THE ICING,** in a medium pan over medium-high heat, melt the butter all the way, then continue cooking until the butter starts to darken and sizzle, about 5 minutes. It should smell nutty and fragrant and turn a beautiful, deep caramel brown. Stay close to the pan while you're doing this; browned butter can go from delicious to burnt in seconds. As soon as the butter has browned, stir in the date molasses—watch out, it may spit and sizzle dramatically—then stir in the confectioners' sugar, ground ginger, and salt and continue stirring until the sugar is fully dissolved and the icing is smooth.

Pour the icing over the hot shortbread as soon as you pull it out of the oven, nudging the icing with the back of a spoon to ensure it covers the entire tray evenly. Gently press the crystallized ginger, dates, and pistachios (if using) into the surface of the icing—they should look like jewels trapped in amber. Allow to cool and set completely before cutting into fingers. The cookies will keep, in an airtight container, for about 3 days at room temperature or up to a week in the refrigerator.

PECAN PIE BARS

ABOUT 24 SMALL BARS

For when you want a pecan pie but don't want to deal with the accompanying pomp and circumstance of pie crust and blind baking—this is a date-filled version that you can slice up and eat with one hand. The filling is less gooey than that of your average pecan pie, but it also has more depth of flavor.

PASTRY BASE

2 cups [280 g] flour

½ cup [60 g] milk powder

1 Tbsp confectioners' sugar

1 tsp salt

14 Tbsp [210 g] butter, at room temperature

1 egg, at room temperature

1 tsp vanilla extract

PECAN FILLING

½ cup [65 g] date sugar

½ cup [105 g] packed light brown sugar

2 Tbsp flour

1 Tbsp butter

1 cup [240 ml] date molasses

3 eggs, lightly beaten

2 cups [240 g] pecan halves

1 tsp vanilla extract

¼ tsp salt

TO MAKE THE PASTRY BASE, in a large bowl, combine the flour, milk powder, confectioners' sugar, and salt, then stir with a fork to aerate and break up any lumps. Add the butter, egg, and vanilla and use a wooden spoon (or your clean hands) to gently combine into a soft, loose dough. Press the dough evenly into the base of a 9 x 13 in [23 x 33 cm] quarter sheet pan and freeze for 30 minutes.

Preheat the oven to 325°F [165°C].

TO MAKE THE FILLING, in a large bowl, combine the date sugar, brown sugar, flour, and butter. Add the date molasses and eggs and whisk until frothy. Add the pecans, vanilla, and salt and stir to thoroughly incorporate. Pour onto the chilled pastry base and spread in an even layer. Bake for 40 minutes, or until the top is firm with a few cracks in it. Let cool completely, then use a sharp knife to cut into bars that are roughly 1 x 3 in [2.5 x 7.5 cm]. The bars will keep, in an airtight container, for about 3 days at room temperature or up to a week in the refrigerator.

CARDAMOM–MANGO TART

DESSERT FOR 4, WITH LEFTOVERS

I am, admittedly, a bit of a mango snob—at least when I'm in the Northeast United States, where hard, tasteless mangoes—like bland chunks of moon rock—reign supreme. Much of my longing is for the perfumed, supersaturated Indian mangoes I grew up with, particularly the regal Alphonso. You can address this issue of lackluster fruit by using dates in your bakes to transform blandness into a vivid, jammy filling, rounding out pale edges and adding depth and complexity. Though this tart lacks the notes of jasmine and pine that make fresh peak-season Alphonsos so hauntingly delicious, the rose and cardamom step in to do some heavy lifting.

My other gift to you is this tart crust: Mixed directly in the baking pan, no rolling or chilling or pre-baking needed, it bakes into a flaky, lightly salted dream.

PASTRY BASE

1½ cups [210 g] flour

1 tsp sugar

½ tsp salt

½ cup [120 ml] olive oil

2 Tbsp whole milk or yogurt

1 tsp rosewater

TOPPING

¾ cup [150 g] sugar

2 Tbsp flour

1 or 2 dried organic rosebuds, crushed to a fine powder (optional)

½ tsp ground cardamom or the crushed seeds of 3 to 5 cardamom pods

¼ tsp salt

2 Tbsp cold salted butter

MANGO FILLING

3 to 5 mangoes (about 1 lb [450 g]), peeled, pitted, and diced

5 dates (about 3½ oz [100 g]), pitted and roughly chopped

1 Tbsp flour

1 tsp rosewater

TO MAKE THE PASTRY BASE, preheat the oven to 425°F [220°C].

In an 8 in [20 cm] square baking pan with high sides (or an 8 in [20 cm] round cake pan with high sides), use a fork to stir together the flour, sugar, and salt.

In a small bowl, whisk together the olive oil, milk, and rosewater. Pour this over the flour mixture and mix together just enough to blend. Using the flat pads of your fingers, press out the dough so that it completely covers the base and sides of the pan and is about ⅛ in

[3 mm] thick all around. It might not reach all the way up the sides—that's fine, as long as it's an even height all around. Try not to overwork the dough.

TO MAKE THE TOPPING, in a medium bowl, combine the sugar, flour, the crushed rosebuds (if using), cardamom, and salt. Using your fingers, rub in the butter until it feels like wet, crumbly sand. Set aside.

TO MAKE THE FILLING, in another medium bowl, combine the mangoes and dates with the flour and rosewater. Arrange the fruit mixture over the base of the tart, then spread a thick layer of the topping over the fruit—don't be skimpy and use it all, even if it seems like a lot. Bake for 35 to 45 minutes, or until the fruit is juicy with hot magma-like bubbles popping lazily under a light golden-brown crust. Serve warmish, with ice cream or whipped cream. It also makes a beautiful breakfast, cold from the refrigerator, and keeps, in an airtight container in the refrigerator, for up to 4 days.

BANOFFEE PIE

ONE 8 IN [20 CM] PIE; DESSERT FOR 8

The banana's highest calling. A dessert that is simultaneously ineffable and a simple matter of stirring and chilling, no oven required.

The filling for this pie is the same toffee sauce that's used in Sticky Toffee Pudding (page 214); use what you have left over here to make that, or just spread it on toast for a very decadent morning treat. Note that the toffee won't fully set up and will be more of a caramel consistency when you slice into the pie, oozing out almost like a sauce.

PIE CRUST

1½ cups [150 g] crushed graham crackers or digestive biscuits

6 Tbsp [85 g] butter, melted

TOFFEE FILLING

1 cup [200 g] packed dark brown sugar

4 Tbsp [55 g] butter

1 cup [240 ml] date molasses

1 cup [240 ml] heavy cream

1 tsp vanilla extract

Pinch of salt

1 or 2 large just-ripe bananas, cut into thin slices

1 cup [240 ml] heavy cream

Cocoa powder, sifted if lumpy, for dusting

TO MAKE THE PIE CRUST, line an 8 in [20 cm] springform pan with parchment paper. In a large bowl, stir together the graham cracker or digestive biscuit crumbs and the butter until combined. Spoon into the prepared springform pan and press down to form an even layer across the bottom of the pan. Refrigerate for 15 minutes while you make the toffee filling.

TO MAKE THE TOFFEE FILLING, in a larger pan than you think you'll need (hot caramel bubbles!), combine the brown sugar and butter and melt over medium heat. When the sugar has just dissolved, add the date molasses and stir until completely combined. While whisking continuously, gradually pour in the heavy cream, watching out for hot bubbles. Remove from the heat and whisk in the vanilla and salt. The toffee should be glossy and thick, with a sheen to it, and dark and viscous like hot fudge. Pour about two-thirds of the filling into the springform pan, spreading it evenly, then refrigerate for at least

1 hour and preferably longer. Reserve the remaining filling for another use. It will keep, tightly covered in the refrigerator, for up to 1 week.

Top the pie by shingling the surface of the chilled filling with thin slices of banana, just overlapping them in order to completely cover the toffee.

Whip the cream until soft peaks form, then spoon an exuberant cloud of whipped cream on top of the banana layer. Return the pie to the refrigerator for at least 1 hour and up to 3. Release the pie from the springform pan, dust with cocoa powder, and serve. Store leftovers, lightly covered with plastic wrap and refrigerated, for up to 2 days.

UPSIDE DOWN DATE & ALMOND CAKE

ONE 9 IN [23 CM] CAKE; DESSERT FOR 8 TO 12

Hello, do you like marzipan? Then this tender, almond-scented cake, with its crackly crust of caramelized dates, may be just the right thing for you. That said, be sure to use almond paste, not marzipan; it's usually available in the baking aisle. As for dates, seek out a soft and squidgy variety, such as Medjools. They will melt slightly into the crunchy sugar topping but still retain a certain structural integrity.

You'll need to use a deep 9 in [23 cm] cake pan or springform pan here, not a layer cake pan—the batter will otherwise overflow as it bakes. If you're using a springform pan, place the cake on a baking sheet before putting it in the oven to capture any escaping butter.

1 cup plus 5 Tbsp [296 g] butter, at room temperature

1¾ cups [350 g] sugar

8 to 10 large soft dates (about 1 lb [455 g]), halved and pitted

7 oz [200 g] almond paste, thinly sliced

1 tsp vanilla extract

1 tsp almond extract (optional)

6 eggs, at room temperature

1 cup [140 g] flour

1½ tsp baking powder

½ tsp salt

Preheat the oven to 325°F [165°C]. Butter a 9 in [23 cm] springform pan, then line the bottom with parchment paper. In a large bowl, combine 5 Tbsp [70 g] of the butter and ½ cup [100 g] of the sugar and beat using a stand mixer until thoroughly combined, then spread in a thick, even layer on the bottom of the prepared pan. Arrange the date halves, cut-side up, in a pleasing pattern on top of the butter mixture.

In a large bowl, combine the remaining 1¼ [250 g] cups of sugar and the almond paste and beat until finely crumbled. It should be the texture of fine sand. (You can also use a food processor or blender for this step.) Add in the remaining 1 cup [226 g] of butter, the vanilla extract, and the almond extract (if using) and beat until light and fluffy and visibly paler. Beat in the eggs, one at a time, making sure each one is thoroughly incorporated before adding the next one and scraping down the sides of the bowl as needed. Don't worry if the mixture looks curdled; it will all come together fine.

In a medium bowl, sift together the flour, baking powder, and salt. Add to the egg and butter mixture and use a rubber spatula or wooden spoon to fold the flour in without knocking the air out of the batter. Gently pour the cake batter into the pan, taking care not to dislodge the dates. Smooth out the top of the batter so it covers everything evenly. Bake for 45 to 65 minutes, or until the top is a deep even brown and feels set when you lightly touch the center. A cake tester should come out clean.

Let the cake cool in the pan on a wire rack for 10 to 15 minutes, then release the sides of the springform pan. Run a knife around the sides if it needs a little encouragement and invert the cake onto a serving platter. Serve warm or at room temperature. The cake will keep, lightly wrapped, in a cool spot, for 3 to 4 days, with the marzipan flavor growing more pronounced over time.

OLIVE OIL CAKE WITH RASPBERRY-HIBISCUS GLAZE

ONE 9 IN [23 CM] CAKE; DESSERT
FOR 10 TO 12

This is a low-lying, unassuming cake, dressed up in a glossy lipstick-pink cloak—a real balancing act between everyday snacking cake and Fashion Week glam. Texturally, it's super moist, due to a potent hygroscopic combination of oil, yogurt, and date sugar. That date sugar does double duty, adding beautifully rounded notes of caramel and baking up less sweet than white or brown sugar. You are also using enough olive oil that you'll be able to taste it, particularly after the cake has had a day or so to rest, so please use something you like the flavor of.

Date sugar can be substituted for granulated sugar at a 1:1 ratio in most baking recipes, but if you do this, decrease the amount of flour you use by 25 percent, since date sugar is also absorbent.

Zest of 2 limes
½ cup [100 g] granulated sugar
2 cups [280 g] flour
1 cup [130 g] date sugar
1 tsp salt
½ tsp baking soda
½ tsp baking powder
1 cup [240 ml] olive oil
1½ cups [360 ml] full-fat plain yogurt
3 large eggs
¼ cup [60 ml] fresh lime juice
Raspberry-Hibiscus Glaze
(recipe follows)

Preheat the oven to 325°F [165°C]. Line a 9 in [23 cm] springform pan with parchment paper.

In a large bowl, use your fingers to rub the lime zest into the granulated sugar to release the citrus oils. Stir in the flour, date sugar, salt, baking soda, and baking powder. In another large bowl, whisk together the olive oil, yogurt, eggs, and lime juice. Add this mixture to the flour mixture and whisk until just combined. Pour the batter into the prepared cake pan and bake for 50 to 70 minutes, or until golden brown and set in the center when pierced with a cake tester.

While the cake is baking, make the raspberry-hibiscus glaze. Glaze the cake once it is fully cool. The cake will keep, lightly wrapped or under a cake dome, for 1 to 2 days.

CONT'D

RASPBERRY– HIBISCUS GLAZE

The trio of flavorings here—rose, lime, and hibiscus—all work in service of the raspberry. You shouldn't really be able to tease out individual elements, but the lime makes the glaze taste brighter, the hibiscus makes it tangier, and the rose adds an elusive hint of perfume—like you've just picked the berries yourself under the warm summer sun. If you're using peak-season raspberries, you might not need any of these additional flavors. But if you're using frozen or otherwise lackluster fruit, try this trifecta and see what you think.

8 oz [225 g] raspberries

1 Tbsp fresh lime juice

1 tsp dried hibiscus flowers or 1 teabag hibiscus tea

1 tsp cornstarch

2¼ cups [270 g] confectioners' sugar

3 Tbsp butter, at room temperature

1 tsp rosewater (optional)

In a small pan over low heat, cook the raspberries, lime juice, hibiscus flowers, and cornstarch, stirring frequently, until thickened. Squash the berries against the sides of the pan if needed to encourage this behavior. Remove from the heat and strain the raspberry mixture through a fine-mesh sieve set over a large bowl (this can be a taxing process; I apologize in advance!). You should have about ½ cup [120 ml] of raspberry purée; discard the solids. Let cool to room temperature.

Add the confectioners' sugar, butter, and rosewater (if using) to the strained raspberry mixture, then whisk until smooth, hot hot pink, and juicy. Glaze the cooled cake and let set for a few minutes before serving. It should look so shiny you worry you might leave fingerprints on its surface. The glaze is best made immediately before you use it.

BLACK DESERT CAKE

I wanted to riff on Black Forest cake, creating a sort of sideways take, with the forest morphing into an oasis and dates replacing the black cherries. That got me thinking about gahwa, or Arabic coffee, a traditional accompaniment to dates across the Arabian Peninsula, which led to a saffron and cardamom-flavored coffee syrup brushed across each layer of a chocolate cardamom cake. What emerged from this fever dream is a cake that isn't really any-thing like a Black Forest cake at all, but which, with its exuberant shag-rug-pelt of halwa floss and chocolate curls, has some of the same madcap charm dialed all the way up. It makes a splen-did birthday cake.

The cake layers benefit from being baked a day ahead and allowed to rest so their flavors develop. If you do this, soak each layer in the coffee syrup before you set it aside.

CHOCOLATE CARDAMOM CAKE

1⅓ cups [105 g] unsweetened cocoa powder, sifted if lumpy, plus more for dusting

2 eggs plus 1 egg yolk

1¼ cups [300 ml] whole milk

⅔ cup [150 ml] olive oil or neutral vegetable oil

2 cups [400 g] sugar

2½ cups [350 g] flour

1 Tbsp instant coffee powder

2½ tsp baking soda

1¼ tsp baking powder

1 tsp ground cardamom

1 tsp salt

TO ASSEMBLE AND DECORATE

Gahwa Syrup (recipe follows)

Stabilized Whipped Cream (recipe follows)

12 large, soft dates, pitted and halved lengthwise

2 oz [55 g] dark chocolate

Chocolate sprinkles

Halwa floss (pashmak, pişmaniye, Turkish "cotton candy")

TO MAKE THE CAKE, preheat the oven to 350°F [180°C]. Butter two 8 in [20 cm] round cake pans and dust with a tablespoon or so of cocoa powder (or flour).

In a large bowl, combine the eggs, egg yolk, milk, oil, and sugar until well blended. Stir in 1 cup [240 ml] of hot but not boiling water.

In another large bowl, sift together the 1⅓ cups of cocoa powder, flour, instant coffee powder, baking soda, baking powder, cardamom, and salt. Add this mixture to the egg mixture and stir until smooth and fully blended. The batter will be rela-tively runny. Divide the batter evenly between the prepared pans and bake until a cake tester comes out clean and the tops of the cakes spring back when touched, 30 to 45 minutes. Cool the cakes in the pans on a wire rack for 30 minutes, then remove from the pans, level the tops, and brush with generous quantities of the gahwa syrup, potentially multiple times, until the cakes are fully soaked. The cakes should still be warm enough that the syrup is readily absorbed. You might not use all of the syrup, but plan to use at least two-thirds of it, if not more. For best results, allow the cakes to rest overnight at this point.

TO ASSEMBLE AND DECORATE, once the cake layers are soaked, cover the bottom one with a thick layer of the stabilized whipped cream and arrange most of the date halves in concentric circles on top of the cream (save the 8 prettiest date halves for the top of the cake). Pop the top cake layer, cut-side down, on top, then cover the entire cake in a thick, even layer of the stabilized whipped cream. Use a vegetable peeler to produce fat curls of choc-olate to decorate the top and sides.

CONT'D

Add chocolate sprinkles and generous quantities of fluffed-up halwa
floss—really spackle it on, so the cake
looks almost creature-like. The halwa
floss will absorb moisture from the
cream, so try not to dress it too far
in advance of serving. Arrange the
remaining 8 date halves around
the perimeter of the top of the cake.
Serve right away, while the halwa
floss is still exuberant. The cake will
keep, covered in the refrigerator,
for 1 to 2 days—just be prepared for
deflated floss the morning after. It
will still taste divine.

GAHWA SYRUP

ABOUT 1 CUP [240 ML]

1 Tbsp rosewater

Big pinch of saffron (about 15 threads)

½ tsp ground cardamom

½ cup [120 ml] warm coffee, preferably green-roasted gahwa or light-roasted black coffee

½ cup [120 ml] date molasses

In a small bowl, combine the rosewater, saffron, and cardamom. Let stand for 15 minutes for the spices to bloom and infuse the rosewater until it turns the color of the sun. Add the warm coffee and date molasses and whisk until thoroughly combined. The syrup can be made up to 2 days in advance and stored in an airtight container in the refrigerator until the cake is ready for its coffee bath.

STABILIZED WHIPPED CREAM

2 tsp unflavored gelatin powder

3 cups [710 ml] heavy cream

½ cup [60 g] confectioner's' sugar

In a small microwave-safe bowl, whisk together the gelatin and 2 tablespoons of cold water. Let stand for 5 to 10 minutes. Chill your largest bowl in the refrigerator or freezer until cool to the touch, then pour in the heavy cream and confectioners' sugar and whisk until just before soft peaks form.

Microwave the gelatin mixture for about 5 seconds, or until fully liquid. If you don't own a microwave, you can gently heat the mixture on the stovetop until the gelatin melts. While whipping continuously, slowly drizzle the gelatin into the whipped cream and continue whipping until soft peaks form. Use immediately.

DATE BISCUITS of the WORLD

 IMQARET
— MALTA

 KLEICHA
— IRAQ

 KOLOOCHEH
— INDIA

 MA'AMOUL
— BILAD el SHAM

 KOLOMPEH
— IRAN

 MAKROUD
— MOROCCO

 KLAIJA
— SAUDI ARABIA

 KA'AK ASAWER
— PALESTINE

 KA'AK el NAKACHE
— ALGERIA

 CHORAK
— ARMENIA

 PHOINIKOTA
— CYPRUS

 BRÂDJ
— ALGERIA

MAMA REE'S LOUISIANA DATE ROLL

ABOUT 50 PIECES

Barbara, my mother-in-law, makes this date-laden, fudgy candy every year at Christmastime. Back in Lake Charles, Louisiana, her grandmother made it to mark the festive season, and it was always an occasion when it showed up in the candy dish on Mama Ree's coffee table. In Barbara's words:

"Mama Ree was my father's mother, Marie Danley Smith. She never finished school and married at sixteen, but she was artistic in an untaught way (had a Maxfield Parrish print over her mantel) and possessed a restless intelligence. She made ice cream and churned her own butter, baked all our birthday cakes, and taught me how to make fried chicken. If you asked her for a recipe she would only say yes if she loved you, and then it was just a list of ingredients. My mother and I figured out the date roll, but I have never been able to reproduce her graham cracker cake. For breakfast every morning, she drank an ice-cold Coca-Cola on her front porch. Whenever I spent the night this ritual felt so decadent."

1½ cups [200 g] pitted and roughly chopped dates
3 cups [600 g] sugar
1 cup [240 ml] heavy cream
1 cup [120 g] pecan halves, chopped
Pinch of salt

Lay out two sheets of aluminum foil, each about 1 foot [30 cm] long.

In a large, heavy saucepan over low heat, combine the dates, sugar, and heavy cream. Bring to a slow boil, stirring frequently, for about 1 hour, or until the goop darkens, the dates soften and start to blend, and the mixture is at the soft-ball stage: When you drop a bit into ice water it should form a nice ball with a very slightly firm crust. Remove from the heat and stir in the pecans and the salt. Pour half of the mixture out in a long log onto one of the sheets of foil, leaving 1 to 2 in [2.5 to 5 cm] of clearance on either of the short ends. Roll the long sides of the foil over the log, crimp the seam and the short ends, and leave on a hard surface to cool. Repeat with the rest of the goop to make a second log. Let the logs stand overnight to harden.

The next day, cut each log into ½ in [13 mm] pieces of heaven. Per Barbara, "This was the most delicious taste in the world for a little girl who was allegedly allergic to chocolate. I still think it's better than chocolate. People tend to love it or not."

STICKY TOFFEE PUDDING

ONE 10 X 14 IN [25 X 35.5 CM] CAKE; DESSERT FOR 12 TO 16, DEPENDING ON HOW GREEDY YOU'RE ALL FEELING

Sticky. Toffee. Pudding.

1) It is fun to eat.

2) It is fun to say.

I always assumed this was a classic British dessert, but it's actually a Commonwealth dish, originally from Canada, where it was both invented and popularized in the 1960s. There are some delicious regional variants out there: Australian lumberjack cake (crowned with a toasted lid of crunchy coconut) and Canada's Queen Elizabeth cake (with a broiled sticky topping), for starters.

Most sticky toffee pudding recipes don't actually use many dates—a mere 6 ounces [170 g] or so. This recipe crams a full pound [450 g] of dates into a luscious, moist cake, and then doubles down with a very healthy pour of date molasses in the toffee sauce. If you don't have any date molasses handy, increase the brown sugar to 2 cups [400 g] and proceed with the recipe as written. Both the pudding and the sauce benefit from an overnight rest to let the flavors get cozy with each other. Sticky Toffee Pudding is usually served warm or at room temperature but is also very satisfying forked up cold from the refrigerator.

The quantities given make more sauce than you need, but that is a good problem to have—among other things, you can use it to make Banoffee Pie (page 203).

DATE CAKE

1 lb [450 g] dates, pitted

2 tsp baking soda

1 cup [200 g] packed dark brown sugar

½ cup [100 g] granulated sugar

2 eggs

1 tsp vanilla extract

2 cups [280 g] flour

2 tsp baking powder

½ tsp salt

TOFFEE SAUCE

1 cup [200 g] packed dark brown sugar

4 Tbsp [55 g] butter

1 cup [240 ml] date molasses

1 cup [240 ml] heavy cream

1 tsp vanilla extract

Pinch of salt

Vanilla ice cream or whipped cream (optional but why wouldn't you?), for serving

TO MAKE THE DATE CAKE, preheat the oven to 350°F [180°C]. Butter a deep 10 x 14 in [25 by 35.5 cm] baking pan and set aside.

In a heatproof medium bowl, combine the dates and baking soda. Add 2 cups [475 ml] of hot water, just off the boil, and let stand for 5 minutes. (Baking soda helps the dates dissolve and encourages the cake to brown to its characteristic mahogany sheen.)

Meanwhile, in a large bowl, whisk the brown sugar, granulated sugar, eggs, and vanilla until pale and frothy.

Mash the date mixture with a fork (or, better yet, your clean hands) until the dates are a mushy ooze but still retain a few rustic chunks. Add this mixture to the egg mixture and stir until well combined.

In a large bowl, sift the flour and baking powder, then stir in the salt. Add this mixture to the date mixture and very gently fold until just blended.

Pour the batter into the prepared pan and bake on the center rack for 30 to 40 minutes, or until a cake tester comes out clean. Let the cake cool in the pan on a wire rack while you make the sauce.

TO MAKE THE TOFFEE SAUCE, in a larger pan than you think you'll need (hot caramel bubbles!), combine the brown sugar and butter and melt over medium heat. When the sugar has just dissolved, add the date molasses and stir until completely combined. While whisking continuously, gradually pour in the cream, and watch out for bubbles. Remove from the heat and whisk in the vanilla and salt. The toffee sauce should be glossy and thick, with a sheen to it, and dark and viscous like hot fudge.

TO ASSEMBLE, use a wooden skewer or small sharp knife to poke 15 to 25 holes all over the cake. Slowly pour half of the still-warm toffee sauce over the cake and let it absorb. Serve while still warm and gooey or at room temperature, with more warm sauce passed alongside to be drizzled on as your guests wish. A scoop of vanilla ice cream or softly whipped cream would not go amiss.

DIBS HOKEY POKEY

ONE 9 X 11 IN [23 X 28 CM] SHEET

Hokey pokey (a.k.a. honeycomb candy, or cinder toffee) requires 10 minutes of effort for a very delicious treat. Sometimes making candy can feel like a science experiment, except you get to eat your science fair volcano. Baking soda is the secret to this treat's airy texture. While it's usually made with honey or golden syrup, I like to make hokey pokey with date molasses, which undercuts some of the sickly sweetness honeycomb candy can be prone to. It's delicious as is, a delight coated in dark chocolate, and perhaps at its peak when crumbled directly into a freshly churned batch of Date Dibs Ice Cream (page 179).

Because date molasses is already dark brown, you will not be able to tell by sight alone when the caramel mixture is ready. I strongly recommend you use a candy thermometer or an instant-read thermometer to guide you on this journey.

1½ cups [300 g] sugar

¼ cup [60 ml] date molasses

1 Tbsp baking soda, sifted for any lumps

Brush a 12 x 17 in [30.5 by 43 cm] rimmed baking sheet with neutral oil or use cooking spray or a silicone mat.

In a deep, large pan at least 8 in [20 cm] wide and 3 in [7.5 cm] deep, over medium-high heat, bring the sugar, date molasses, and ¼ cup [60 ml] of water to a boil, stirring continuously with a silicone spatula. Turn the heat to medium and cook, without stirring, until a thermometer registers 300°F [150°C]. Remove from the heat, add the baking soda, and stir just until incorporated—it will whoosh up into a puffy, golden cloud. Gently pour the mixture onto the prepared baking sheet; don't try to spread it out once it hits the sheet, as you will knock the air out of it. Let cool completely, then pry up and smash into pieces for serving. Hokey pokey can be stored, in an airtight container at room temperature, for up to a week; be warned that if you keep it in the refrigerator it will soften.

Vyolette
VIOLET

NYM ALMAUNDE MYLKE, AN FLOWRE of RYS, AND POUDER GYNGERE, GALYNGALE, PEPIR, DATIS, FYGYS, & RASONYS Y-CORVEN, AN COLOURE IT WITH SAFROUN, AN BOYLE IT & MAKE IT CHARGEAUNT; AN WHAN ÞOU DRESSYTE, TAKE ÞE FLOWRES, AN HEW HEM, AN STYRE IT ÞER-WITH; NYME ÞE BRAUNCHYS WITH ÞE FLOWRES, AN SETTE A-BOVE AND SERUE IT FORTH.

TAKE ALMOND MILK, AND RICE FLOUR, AND POWDERED GINGER, GALANGAL, PEPPER. CUT DATES, FIGS & RAISINS, AND COLOR WITH SAFFRON. BOIL IT AND MAKE IT THICK. AND WHEN YOU DRESS IT, TAKE FLOWERS & CUT THEM, AND STIR THEM IN; CUT THE BRANCHES WITH THE FLOWERS & SERVE IT FORTH.

a RECIPE from a FIFTEENTH-CENTURY COOKERY-BOOK from ENGLAND

ISPHANA'S SHEER KHURMA

BUCKETS OF FESTIVE BREAK/FAST; ENOUGH FOR 6, WITH LEFTOVERS

When I was a child, the best meal of the year was breakfast on Eid al Fitr, the first daylight meal we could all share after a long month of Ramadan fasting. We would rush downstairs to snag a bowlful of my mother's signature sweet sheer khurma, which she makes in enormous quantities. An assembly line of foil containers would cover all available counter space, waiting to be filled and distributed as a festive treat for the many households on my father's side of the family.

Although my mother grew up eating sheer khurma in Bombay, India, the origins of this sweet are widespread— it emerged somewhere along the Silk Road and is now found across the subcontinent, including in India, Pakistan, Bangladesh, and Afghanistan. Its name is Persian—sheer for "milk" and khurma for "dates." (As a side note, one of my favorite etymologies is seersucker: sheer for "milk" and shakar for "cream," so milk and cream, for the alternating woven stripes.) Think of a very soupy rice pudding, then swap out the rice for vermicelli, crushed into short lengths, and add copious quantities of warm spices, nuts, and dried fruit, particularly kharak-style dried dates (see The Many Forms of the Date on page 30 for more on dried dates).

Per my mother, "Like biryani, each family has its own recipe for sheer khurma, passed down from one generation to the next. Besides the cardamom and saffron, people also use desiccated coconut, chironji [an almond-like seed], and rosewater as flavoring. Occasionally, I add soaked raisins as a garnish. As kids, we all loved sheer khurma, and since it was only cooked on the Eids in our household, it was something we all looked forward to enjoying during these festivities.

"I remember my grandmother making a special trip to the dried fruit store (nuts and dates were not available in regular stores in those days) to make sure all the ingredients were appropriately bought in time and in the right amounts to make the dish in a huge vessel. She personally supervised the cook to ensure it was made to her satisfaction. My cousins and I would watch the proceedings with great interest because we all just loved to eat it! On Eid mornings we would all enjoy a hot bowl of the dessert. My grandmother would keep the rest to serve to Eid visitors, but we kids all had our eyes on it and would look for an opportunity to grab more. I particularly savored the taste of it eaten cold the next day. I found it quite special!"

8 cups [1.9 L] whole milk

6 Tbsp [50 g] sugar

4 big pinches of saffron

3 tsp ground cardamom

½ cup [35 g] vermicelli, broken into small pieces

1 cup [120 g] blanched slivered almonds

1 cup [120 g] pistachios, slivered

1 cup [100 g] kharak (dried dates), soaked overnight and thinly sliced

In a large saucepan or stock pot set over medium-high heat, bring the milk, sugar, saffron, and cardamom to a boil. Turn the heat to low, then stir in the vermicelli and simmer until cooked through, 6 to 7 minutes. Add the almonds, pistachios, and dried dates and cook until the milk is slightly thickened, 5 to 10 minutes. Remove from the heat and let rest for about 20 minutes to let the flavors marry. Serve hot. Leftovers can be stored in an airtight container and refrigerated for up to 5 days and served cold; much like next-day pizza or kunafa, I find it makes a very decadent breakfast straight from the refrigerator, particularly when Eid falls during the summertime.

MABROOSHEH

ABOUT 25 SMALL SQUARES

A traditional teatime snack baked widely across the Middle East, this jam tart is the sort of thing you can whip up at a moment's notice. It's unglamorous but thoroughly soothing. You can use any type of jam you have lying around, but date and apricot are the two I've seen most often. *Mabroosheh* means "grated" in Arabic and is a reference to the chilled dough that you grate to form a top crust, which bakes into crunchy, buttery nubbins in the oven. This is a particularly fun and easy baked good to make with any children who can be trusted to create a minimum amount of chaos with a grater.

2 cups [280 g] flour

½ cup [60 g] milk powder

1 Tbsp confectioners' sugar

1 tsp salt

14 Tbsp [210 g] butter, at room temperature

1 egg, at room temperature

1 tsp vanilla extract

1 cup [300 g] date jam (store-bought or One-Ingredient Date Jam, page 238)

In a large bowl, combine the flour, milk powder, confectioners' sugar, and salt, then stir with a fork to aerate and break up any lumps. Add the butter, egg, and vanilla and use a wooden spoon (or your clean hands) to gently combine into a soft, loose dough. Divide the dough in half. Put one half in the freezer for 15 to 20 minutes. Press the remaining half evenly into the base of an 8 in [20 cm] square baking pan, then freeze for 15 minutes.

Preheat the oven to 350°F [180°C].

Remove the pan from the freezer and spread a generous layer of date jam across the dough. Remove the rest of the dough from the freezer and use the large holes of a box grater to grate the dough directly on top of the jam. Try to get a relatively even layer of coverage, but a few wiggles are fine—it should look a little free-form.

Bake until the dough is fragrant and pale golden brown, 20 to 35 minutes (a wide window; keep checking!). Let cool completely before slicing and serving. Mabroosheh will keep, covered, at room temperature for up to 3 days.

DATE MA'AMOUL

Dates are used to stuff and sweeten pastries across the globe. One of the varieties nearest to my heart is ma'amoul (also called ka'ak or kahk), a date-stuffed biscuit made across the Middle East by members of the major religious groups. It's a beloved celebration food for Eid, Easter, and Purim. There's a long regional history: Similar pastries can be traced back to Mesopotamia and ancient Egypt, where they were stamped with the symbol of the sun god, Ra. These days, wooden ma'amoul molds are often passed down from one generation to the next. Making ma'amoul is a family affair, after all: It takes many hands to shape and stuff the dough with the traditional fillings of dates, walnuts, or pistachios.

Deep in Bay Ridge, Brooklyn, I was delighted to find that a couple of Middle Eastern grocery stores stocked ma'amoul molds for sale alongside mooncake molds—whatever it takes to get the job done. If you can't find anything that suits, a fork or pair of tweezers is enough to make a pretty pattern. Whether homemade or store-bought, ma'amoul are commonly given as gifts. During the Fatimid dynasty in the eleventh century CE, the baking and distribution of Eid ma'amoul (some stuffed with secret gold coins, like Willy Wonka on steroids) was such a logistically complex operation that a separate government department was created to ensure that the caliph's largesse was appropriately bestowed.

1½ cups [210 g] flour

½ cup [115 g] butter, cut into small pieces

1 Tbsp orange blossom water

1 Tbsp rosewater

2 to 3 Tbsp milk

½ lb [225 g] date paste

Confectioners' sugar, for sprinkling

In a large bowl, use your fingertips to blend together the flour and butter. Add the orange blossom water and the rosewater and just enough milk to bring it all together, and work into a soft, pliable dough. You may not need to use all the milk here.

Pinch off a piece of dough about the size of a walnut, and roll into a sphere. Then, use your thumb to hollow out the center of it. Take a smaller piece of date paste, roll into a ball the size of a large marble, and place inside the hollow—it should be about ¾ full, not overflowing. Gently roll the dough around the date paste ball so that it is completely covered, then flatten ever so slightly. If using a ma'amoul mold, pop the filled dough ball in, press down so it fills the mold, then rap the mold firmly in order to release. If you don't have a mold, use tweezers or a sharp fork to make decorative swirls and dots—you want some nooks and crannies for the confectioners' sugar to settle into after the pastries have baked and cooled. Put the ma'amoul in the refrigerator for around 30 minutes to ensure the designs don't become blurry when baked.

Preheat the oven to 325°F [165°C]. Bake the ma'amoul for 20 to 25 minutes. Keep an eye on them: if they brown at all, they will become tough. The dough will still feel soft and almost uncooked while warm, but it will firm up on cooling. Allow to cool completely, then dust with a blizzard of confectioners' sugar. They'll keep well for weeks at room temperature in a tightly sealed tin.

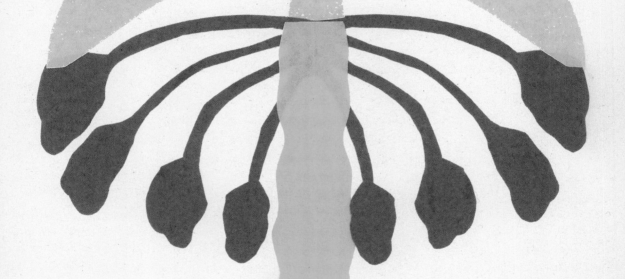

DRINKS
&
CONDIMENTS

PALM SPRINGS DATE SHAKE

1 LARGE SHAKE

The quintessential Coachella Valley recipe, this shake is a celebration of the California Medjool—more than 90 percent of the dates grown in the United States come from around Palm Springs. It's a true milkshake, not a smoothie: very sweet and decadent, with the dates providing almost more of a texture than a taste—delicious little flecks of skin and fibrous date flesh. Some roadside stands thin out their shakes, and others blend their version so thick you need to use a spoon instead of a mere drinking straw.

You can use ¼ cup [40 g] of date crystals in place of the Medjools if you want to be super faithful to the Palm Springs version; just soak in warm water as you would the chopped dates.

3 Medjool dates, pitted and finely chopped

¼ cup [60 ml] whole milk, as cold as possible

1 cup [235 g] vanilla ice cream

In a small bowl, soak the chopped dates in ¼ cup [60 ml] of hot water for about 10 minutes, then chill in the refrigerator until cool.

In a blender, blend the dates, their soaking water, and the milk until smooth and frothy. Add the ice cream and pulse until just blended. Serve cold.

DESERT HOT SPRINGS

SKY VALLEY

SAM COBB DATE FARMS

TWO BUNCH PALMS

10

NORTH PALM SPRINGS

WINDMILL MARKET

THOUSAND PALMS

DA... CH...

COACHELLA

10

86

INDIO

DATE MUSEUM

111

NATIONAL DATE FESTIVAL

HADLEY'S DATE GARDENS

FRESH DATES BY ANDERSON

RANCHO AZIZ

THERMAL

OASIS DATE GARDENS

FLYING DISC RANCH

MECCA BAUTISTA'S FAMILY ORGANIC DATES

111

SALTON SEA

PATO'S DREAM DATE GARDEN

CANDY'S DREAM DATES

REGULUS RANCH

OASIS

SHOP(PE) ICE CREAM

WORKSHOP TRIO

BAR CECIL

533 VIET FUSION

111

111

PALM SPRINGS

SHIELDS DATE GARDEN

PALM DESERT

74

ROMANCE Theatre

free CONTINUOUS

ROMANCE AND SEX LIFE
OF THE DATE

DATE SHAKES

GROCERIES — PRODUCE

Takeout Meals

Original DATE SHAKE

SHIELDS
SINCE 1924

DONT MISS IT!

OPEN ALL YEAR

GREATER PALM SPRINGS and
the COACHELLA VALLEY

WIND FARMS. SAND DUNES. WHEN I ARRIVED in EARLY MARCH, EVERYONE WANTED TO TELL ME ABOUT the HABOOB I HAD JUST MISSED — A SAND-TSUNAMI THAT HIT LIKE A TRAIN, WHITEOUT CONDITIONS. THE AIR the NEXT DAY FILLED WITH SUSPENDED PARTICLES. THE TERM HABOOB, of course, FROM the ARABIC for A VIOLENT WIND. THE WEATHER EVENTS, the LANDSCAPE so similar to the PLACE I GREW UP & so VASTLY DISTINCT. THE AREA from the SALTON SEA to Mt. SAN JACINTO, FED BY ARTESIAN WELLS & the ALL-AMERICAN CANAL, CHANNELING PRECIOUS WATER FROM the COLORADO RIVER, HUNDREDS of MILES AWAY. THE MARCH RAINS HAD JUST PASSED & the DESERT WAS IN BLOOM, YELLOW & PURPLE FLOWERS CARPETING the VALLEY FLOOR. TINY PINPRICKS of COLOR on A VAST SCALE. AND EVERYWHERE, DATE FARMS: ROADSIDE SIGNS ALONG HIGHWAY 111, the "DATE PALM HIGH-WAY", AND GROVES of ELEGANT PALMS PRODUCING ENORMOUS FRUIT ON AN ENORMOUS AMERICAN SCALE: OVER 90% of the DATES GROWN in the...

DatePalm Drive — EXIT 126

RINGED BY SNOWCAPPED MOUNTAINS, the COACHELLA VALLEY IS NESTLED RIGHT UP to the SAN ANDREAS FAULT — GREAT CRACKS in the GROUND BRISTLING WITH NATIVE FAN PALMS, SHAGGY BEARDED. HUDDLES DRINKING DEEP from THERMAL SPRINGS. THE TOWNS HAVE NAMES WITH FLAVORS of the "EXOTIC ORIENT" — MECCA, OASIS, THERMAL, THOUSAND PALMS — RELICS of the COLONIZING INFLUENCE of the DATE PALMS THAT WERE BROUGHT HERE from NORTH AFRICA OVER A CENTURY AGO BY "ADVENTURERS" SUBSIDIZED by the US DEPARTMENT of AGRICULTURE — DETERMINED to MAKE the DESERT COMMERCIALLY VIABLE. THEY BROUGHT OVER CAMELS, TOO, BUT the CAMELS HAD OPINIONS and FAILED to THRIVE.

a chair at Sheikh's Date Garden

ON the MENU

A GREATER PALM SPRINGS SAMPLER

SIGNATURE DATE BURGER
TOPPED WITH SAUTÉED DEGLET NOOR DATES, BACON, AND MELTED BLEU CHEESE
SHIELDS DATE GARDEN

TRIO COACHELLA VALLEY DATES
AZIZ FARMS MEDJOOL DATES | BACON WRAPPED | GORGONZOLA CREAM CHEESE | ROASTED DILL JALAPEÑO AÏOLI

DATE SHAKE
COACHELLA VALLEY MEDJOOL DATES, BANANA, ALMOND BUTTER, ALMOND MILK, ESPRESSO SHOT
TWO BUNCH PALMS

LOCAL LEMON TART
WHIPPED CREAM, DATE PUREÉ, PISTACHIO
BAR CECIL

"BEST DATE SHAKE in the DESERT"
WINDMILL MARKET

CECIL'S BREAD ROLLS
WITH LOCAL DATE + SAGE BUTTER
BAR CECIL

SHOP (PE)

COACHELLA VALLEY DATE ICE CREAM

533 VIET FUSION

MAINE LOBSTER CLAW SPRING ROLL WITH WATERCRESS, PEA SHOOTS, DATES, BUCKWHEAT NOODLES, CILANTRO HONEY DIPPING SAUCE

1. INDIAN ROLLER • 2 • CARACAL • 3 • OASIS SKIMMER • 4 • LESSER JERBOA •
5 • ARABIAN HORNED VIPER • 6 • ARABIAN DARKLING BEETLE • 7 • ARABIAN
SAND GAZELLE • 8 • BRANDTS HEDGEHOG • 9 • DESERT HEDGEHOG • 10 • ORYX •
11 • ARABIAN SAND FISH or SKINK • 12 • CROWNED LEAF-NOSE SNAKE • 13 • DHUB or
SPINY-TAILED LIZARD • 14 • JAYAKARS SAND BOA • 15 • SAND FOX • 16 • EGYPTIAN FRUITBAT •
17 • SULPHOROUS JEWEL BEETLE • 18 • GREATER HOOPOE-LARK • 19 • ARABIAN or DESERT HARE •

9.

13.

14.

15.

10.

18.

16.

17.

19.

DATE PALMS THRIVE

in OASES, FERTILE AREAS

POLKA-DOTTED THROUGHOUT DESERTS & OTHER ARID LANDS.

OASES ARE OFTEN IRRIGATED by SPRINGS or UNDERGROUND WELLS, & the WATER ATTRACTS

PLANT & ANIMAL LIFE. HERE ARE SOME ANIMALS of ABU DHABI'S LIWA OASIS, an ANCIENT YET

STILL-THRIVING OASIS CUPPING the NORTHERNMOST RIM of the RUB al-KHALI, or EMPTY QUARTER—the

LARGEST SAND DESERT in the WORLD. The SOOTHING GREEN DATE GROVES STRIKE a CONTRAST with the

SURROUNDING RED DUNES.

WILD DATES KNEADED WITH LOCUSTS and Spices

"FIND a SWARM of LOCUSTS RESTING AFTER a LONG FLIGHT and GATHER THEM in a COVERED BASKET. UNDER the SHADE of a DATE PALM, CAREFULLY PICK OUT and DISCARD the DEAD LOCUSTS. PLACE the LIVE ONES in a LARGE BOWL, ADD the WATER and SALT to DROWN THEM, then DRAIN OFF the WATER and RETURN the LOCUSTS to the BASKET. [BRINE the LOCUSTS in a SOLUTION of ROSEWATER & SALT, SPICED with CORIANDER, FENNEL and ASAFOETIDA. DRAIN, THEN FERMENT TWO WEEKS].

TRANSFER the LOCUSTS to a LARGE BOWL, ADD DATES, and KNEAD them TOGETHER with YOUR HANDS UNTIL FULLY COMBINED and a SOFT MIXTURE HAS FORMED. PAT INTO DISK-LIKE CAKES. STORE IN a SADDLEBAG of CAMEL LEATHER."

A NOMADIC ARABIAN DESERT RECIPE from "CUMIN, CAMELS, and CARAVANS," by GARY NABHAN, himself inspired by IBN SAYYĀR al WARRĀQ's "KITAB al-TABĪKH", the earliest known Arabic-language cookbook from 10th-century CE Baghdad.

YOU ARE LIKE A **PALM TREE** in the MIND:

NEITHER STORM NOR WOODSMAN'S AX CAN FELL IT.

ITS BRAIDS UNCUT
BY the BEASTS of DESERT and FOREST

BUT I AM the EXILED ONE BEHIND WALL and DOOR,

SHELTER ME in the **WARMTH** of YOUR GAZE.

from "A LOVER from PALESTINE"
by MAHMOUD DARWISH

STICKY DATE MASALA CHAI

CHAI FOR 4

Every time it rains in Dubai, a bona fide desert, my mother gets a wistful look on her face and reminisces about the childhood pleasure of drinking chai during monsoon season in India—a steaming hot cup served with platters of just-fried pakoras.

Sticky chai is an Australian invention, as far as I can tell, a ready-to-go concoction of honey or another syrupy sweetener—I like to use date molasses for its caramel undertones—with black tea and warming spices. Tailor the spice blend to suit your tastes. I prefer mine heavy on ginger and don't want cloves anywhere near my chai, but you may feel otherwise. Other options to consider: pink peppercorns, whole fennel seeds, ground turmeric, saffron, rose petals, vanilla bean pods, star anise . . .

To make one serving of chai, use 1 to 2 tablespoons of the masala. To make four servings, use the whole batch. I use a one-to-one ratio of milk to water to make my chai; if you prefer yours creamier, use more milk than water.

3 Tbsp loose-leaf black tea, the stronger the better (I like Assam)

15 cardamom pods, lightly cracked with the flat of a knife or mortar and pestle but otherwise left whole, or 1 Tbsp ground cardamom

2 Tbsp ground ginger

2 tsp ground cinnamon or 2 cinnamon sticks, broken into small pieces

1 tsp whole black peppercorns

3 Tbsp date molasses, plus more if needed

2 cups [475 ml] milk (I use whole cow's milk, but you can use any kind you like)

To make the chai masala, in a medium bowl, combine the tea, cardamom, ginger, cinnamon, peppercorns, and date molasses. Use a spatula to mix everything together until it is the texture of a wet, syrupy granola—you may need to dig around to make sure there aren't any pockets of dry mix hiding from you. Add another spoonful of date molasses if needed. Use immediately, or store the masala in a jar in the refrigerator for up to a month.

To make the chai, in a small saucepan, combine ½ cup [120 ml] of water and ½ cup [120 ml] of milk, along with a tablespoon or two of masala for every mug of tea you want to make. Bring to a rolling boil, stirring or swirling as needed. Watch your tea carefully—it will boil over sneakily the moment your attention wanders. You are going to bring it to a boil three times, which will aerate the chai and encourage it to develop its signature luscious and creamy texture. Each time, allow the chai to foam up to just below the lip of the pan, then pull it off the heat and swirl it gently until the tea subsides. Return to the heat and repeat until the tea has foamed and subsided twice more. Strain into a cup or mug and enjoy; you may find that the quantity of liquid has reduced and thickened, which is good. Best served on a gray day, with rain pattering against the window.

WINTER ELIXIR

1 SMALL JAR OF PASTE, ABOUT 6 SERVINGS

A little jar of this business is a lovely gift for someone who is feeling under the weather. Back when we all went into the office every day, I used to keep a jar of elixir at my desk for cold and flu season.

2 tsp ground turmeric

1 tsp ground ginger

½ tsp ground cinnamon

½ tsp freshly ground black pepper

½ tsp coconut oil or olive oil

⅓ cup [80 ml] date molasses

A big squeeze of lemon, for serving

In a small bowl, work the turmeric, ginger, cinnamon, pepper, and oil into the date molasses until it forms a paste. You can mix this directly in the jar and keep it handy through the coldest days of the winter. It will keep indefinitely at room temperature.

Stir 1 teaspoon of paste into a mug of hot but not boiling water and add a hearty squeeze of fresh lemon juice to taste.

NOTE: You can also use this to make a sort of haldi doodh/golden milk: Heat up a mug of the milk of your choice, then stir in a teaspoon of elixir paste; omit the lemon. For another variation, use brewed black tea as your base and top it up with a shot of bourbon for a warming hot toddy–esque situation.

JALLAB

2 ICY GLASSES (MULTIPLIES EASILY)

My god, a glass of jallab on a hot day, the sun beating down on the warm green water of the Arabian Gulf, the air so heavy with humidity you could mold it like playdough. The sort of day you see mirages on the highway, phantom puddles of water shivering above the asphalt. A day so hot the sky turns white, not blue, and you wish you had a second pair of sunglasses to slide over the ones you're already wearing. Everything gets slower, your thoughts a little loosey-goosey. That's the kind of day that calls for jallab. A tall glass sweaty with crushed ice, a long straw you use to fish around for the pine nuts and the raisins at the bottom of the glass. A little floral, dark and sweet, gloriously refreshing.

3 Tbsp date molasses (you can also use a 1:1 mixture of date and grape molasses)

1 tsp rosewater

Lots of crushed ice

2 Tbsp pine nuts

2 Tbsp golden raisins

In a pitcher, combine the date molasses, rosewater, and 3 cups [710 ml] of cool water and stir until thoroughly mixed. Fill two tall glasses with crushed ice and pour in the jallab mixture. Top each glass with 1 tablespoon of pine nuts and 1 tablespoon of raisins. Serve with straws. Stay cool.

ONE-INGREDIENT DATE JAM

ABOUT 2 CUPS [500 G]

This is a very easy and very quick jam to whizz up whenever you need it—the only ingredient, aside from water, is dates. You can, of course, add other flavorings (thick curls of lemon peel, a big pinch of saffron, the spent husk of a vanilla bean) or use another liquid (coffee!), but at its simplest, this is a beautiful expression of the natural sweetness and complexity of the date. Try it with Medjools or Deglet Nours, but it's also a lovely vehicle for other varieties—consider Sukkaris for a jam that tastes almost like salted caramel, or Ajwas for a jam with a raisin-like, molasses-y quality. You can substitute this for date paste in many of the recipes in this book, but it will be much thinner and waterier than store-bought, so be aware you might need to do some tweaking to the as-written recipe quantities.

10 to 12 Medjool dates or 15 to 20 smaller dates (about 9 oz [255 g]), pitted

Pinch of salt (optional)

In a smallish, high-sided pan over medium heat, combine the dates and 1 cup [240 ml] of water and bring to a simmer. Continue simmering, stirring occasionally, for 3 to 5 minutes. Once the dates begin to disintegrate and get a little loosey-goosey around the edges, remove from the heat and blend until smooth and creamy. I prefer to use an immersion blender to pulse the jam directly in the pan, but you can also transfer the mixture to a regular blender and then back to the pan.

Turn the heat to medium-low and continue to cook the blended mixture, stirring frequently, until thick and jammy—another 5 to 7 minutes. Use a silicone spatula to scrape down the sides and bottom of the pan. The jam is ready when your spatula leaves a clear trail on the base of the pan and the jam smells lightly caramelized. Taste and see if you want to add a little bit of salt to heighten the complexity of flavor. Let the jam cool, then transfer to a clean jar. It will keep, refrigerated, for up to a week.

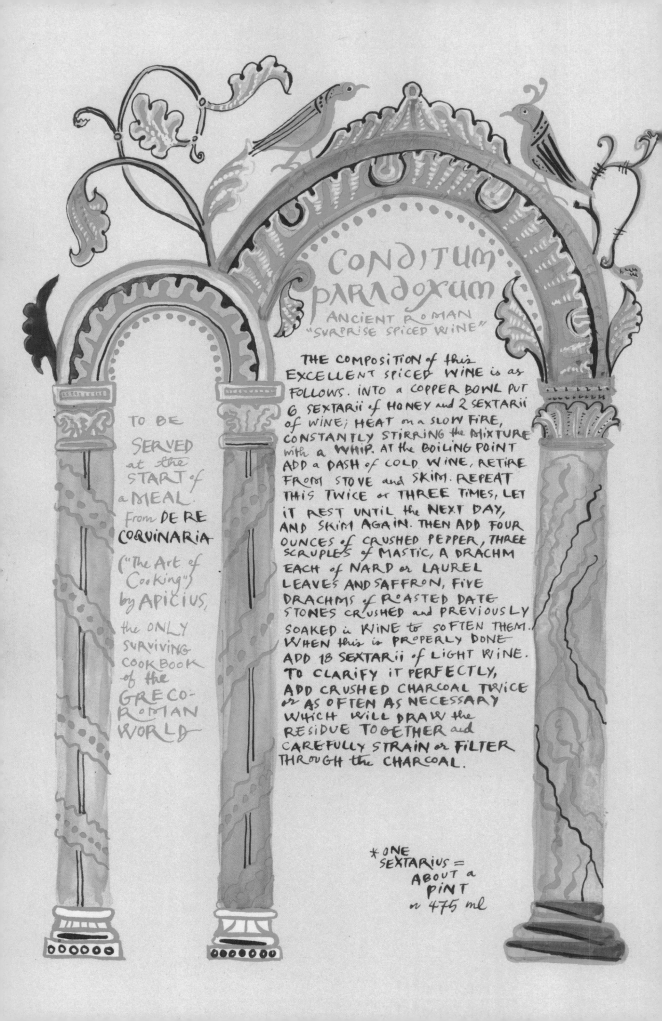

CONDITUM PARADOXUM

ANCIENT ROMAN "SURPRISE SPICED WINE"

TO BE SERVED at the START of a MEAL. From DE RE COQUINARIA ("The Art of Cooking") by APICIUS, the ONLY SURVIVING COOKBOOK of the GRECO-ROMAN WORLD

THE COMPOSITION of this EXCELLENT SPICED WINE is as FOLLOWS. INTO a COPPER BOWL PUT 6 SEXTARII of HONEY and 2 SEXTARII of WINE; HEAT on a SLOW FIRE, CONSTANTLY STIRRING the MIXTURE with a WHIP. AT the BOILING POINT ADD a DASH of COLD WINE, RETIRE FROM STOVE and SKIM. REPEAT THIS TWICE or THREE TIMES, LET IT REST UNTIL the NEXT DAY, AND SKIM AGAIN. THEN ADD FOUR OUNCES of CRUSHED PEPPER, THREE SCRUPLES of MASTIC, A DRACHM EACH of NARD or LAUREL LEAVES AND SAFFRON, FIVE DRACHMS of ROASTED DATE STONES CRUSHED and PREVIOUSLY SOAKED in WINE to SOFTEN THEM. WHEN this is PROPERLY DONE ADD 18 SEXTARII of LIGHT WINE. TO CLARIFY IT PERFECTLY, ADD CRUSHED CHARCOAL TWICE or AS OFTEN AS NECESSARY WHICH WILL DRAW the RESIDUE TOGETHER and CAREFULLY STRAIN or FILTER THROUGH the CHARCOAL.

*ONE SEXTARIUS = ABOUT a PINT or 475 ml

YOUR EYES ARE STANDS of DATE PALMS PRE-DAWN
OR BALCONIES the MOON DRAWS AWAY FROM

WHEN YOUR EYES SMILE the VINES SHOOT LEAVES
AND the LIGHTS DANCE... LIKE MOONS in a RIVER
DISTURBED TREMULOUSLY BY AN OAR PRE-DAWN

AS if WHAT THROBBED in THEIR DEPTHS WERE the STARS
AND THEY SINK in a FOG of TRANSPARENT BEREAVEMENT
LIKE the SEA COMBED OVER by the HANDS of EVENING...

from RAIN SONG by
BADR SHAKIR AL-SAYYAB,
trans. COLBY SOMERVILLE

A CONDIMENT TO CURE WHAT AILS YOU

ABOUT 2 CUPS [480 G]

This recipe is based on Foriana sauce, a Sicilian wonder-condiment that combines nuts, herbs, dried fruit, and garlic to miraculous effect. You can switch up the nuts here, but don't use too many hard nuts, like almonds, and be sure to mix in a few softies, like walnuts, pecans, or pine nuts. This stuff is magical. It's sweet, salty, and garlicky, and it makes everything it touches a million times tastier.

Try the condiment on seedy toasts spread with clouds of ricotta, tossed with quick-blanched Swiss chard (dates + swiss chard = a winning combo), swirled through angel hair pasta with a snowfall of Parmesan, in a savory morning yogurt bowl with some diced tomatoes and scallions, spooned on top of lightly poached cod, or tucked under the skin of a chicken that you roast so that its delicious chickeny juices combine with the condiment's magical garlicky ways to yield crisp skin and tender meat . . .

1 cup [140 g] raw walnut halves

1 cup [120 g] combined, any blend of pistachios, pepitas, pine nuts, almonds, cashews, and/or sunflower seeds (I like a Tbsp or so of sesame seeds in the mix too)

10 plump garlic cloves, sliced as thinly as possible

3 tsp dried oregano

3 Tbsp olive oil, plus more to cover

½ cup [75 g] finely chopped dates

Salt

In a food processor or a mortar and pestle, grind the walnuts, pistachios, garlic, and oregano until they are a nutty rubble: You want tiny pebbles, not sand.

In a medium skillet or sauté pan over medium heat, warm the olive oil. Add the nut mixture, dates, and salt and toast, stirring continuously, until the mixture is golden brown—about 5 minutes. Don't let the nuts burn, but make sure all your garlic is cooked through.

Fill a clean pint jar with the cooked mixture. Pour over enough fresh olive oil to cover the surface each time you use it; this will help to keep it preserved. The condiment will keep, in the refrigerator, for up to 10 days, but I guarantee you will have eaten it all long before then.

JAMMY CHILI DATE OIL

ABOUT 2 CUPS [480 G]

This is a rambunctious, earthy chili oil, textured with slow-cooked shallot and garlic, brightened with an electric thrum of Sichuan pepper, and punctuated throughout with sweet fragments of date. It plays as well with a stovetop-charred pita and a puddle of labneh for breakfast as it does surrounded by a moat of soy sauce and vinegar to liven up a dinner of dumplings scavenged from your emergency freezer stash. Take your time when it comes to mincing the garlic and shallot and use your knife skills—you'll feel the difference in texture on your tongue.

I like firm Deglet Nour dates here, but any kind will do.

As recipes go, this is a very forgiving one. You can adjust the blend of chili flakes to suit the level of heat you're interested in; the ones I've recommended are always in my pantry and make for a very flavorful but relatively mild burn. Calibrate to your own tastes: If you want more earthiness, add more mushroom powder. More smoke? Add paprika. More heat? Change up the chili flakes for something punchier, or go much harder on the Sichuan and white peppers.

1 cup [240 ml] mild olive oil or neutral oil, such as grapeseed or canola

6 garlic cloves, minced

1 cup [50 g] minced shallots

9 to 11 dates, pitted and finely chopped

¼ cup [25 g] gochugaru (coarse Korean hot pepper flakes) or other flaky, fruity, and relatively mild chili flakes

2 Tbsp mild red chili flakes, such as Aleppo or Urfa biber

1 tsp sweet smoked paprika

1 tsp salt

½ tsp dried mushroom or MSG powder (optional, to add umami)

1 tsp ground Sichuan pepper

1 tsp ground white pepper

In a deep, medium saucepan over medium heat, warm the oil. Add the garlic, shallots, dates, gochugaru, chili flakes, paprika, salt, and mushroom or MSG powder (if using) and cook (the mixture may foam up), stirring, until the garlic and shallots turn light golden brown, up to 5 minutes. Turn the heat to low and continue cooking, stirring every few minutes to prevent burning, until the oil turns a beautiful reddish-brown and the ingredients are almost dry. This can take anywhere from 15 to 30 minutes. Don't be tempted to turn the heat up

and rush this process or you'll burn the garlic and be left with a bitter rubble in a noxious, oily sea. Remove from the heat and stir in the Sichuan pepper and white pepper. Let the mixture cool, then transfer it to a clean pint jar. The chili oil is ready right away, but gets better over time. It will keep in the refrigerator for up to a week, but you will have eaten it all long before then.

SPICED DATE CHILI CRISP

ABOUT 2 CUPS [480 G]

Does anyone need another chili crisp recipe in their lives? Probably not! Will this specific one, with sweet chewy dates rumbling alongside a boisterous tangle of crispy onions and golden garlic chips, a veritable symphony of spices, citrus zests, and umami-boosting mushroom powder, plus the rich crunch of almonds and pumpkin seeds, change your life maybe a little bit? Probably yes!

This chili crisp is the ideal companion for a bacon-y breakfast sandwich, but if you need other ideas for what to do with it, try stirring it into noodles or spooning it over rice and sautéed greens. It is a beautiful topping for a sunny-side up egg, makes avocado toast shine, and adds crunch and fire when used to top a bowl of soup (try it with Double-Ginger Carrot Soup, page 150). My favorite way to use this chili crisp, though, is to spread it thickly onto a slab of sheep's milk feta, shingle that with thinly sliced fresh figs, and bake in the oven at 350°F [180°C] until the cheese turns soft and custardy but still retains its shape. Serve with crackers as the perfect party food.

3 Tbsp mild red chili flakes, such as Urfa biber or gochugaru

1 Tbsp spicier chili powder, such as Kashmiri chili

1 Tbsp nutritional yeast (optional)

½ Tbsp sweet smoked paprika

1 tsp orange zest

1 tsp sugar

1 tsp whole cumin seeds

1 tsp ground turmeric

½ tsp ground cinnamon

½ tsp whole fennel seeds

½ tsp salt

½ tsp dried mushroom or MSG powder (optional, to add umami)

1 cup [240 ml] olive oil

6 garlic cloves, sliced into paper-thin chips

One 2 in [5 cm] piece fresh ginger, peeled and finely minced

¼ cup [30 g] slivered almonds, roughly chopped

¼ cup [25 g] raw unsalted pepitas, roughly chopped

3 Tbsp store-bought crispy fried shallots

8 Deglet Nour dates or other firm, chewy dates, pitted and finely chopped

In a small bowl, stir together the chili flakes, chili powder, nutritional yeast (if using), paprika, orange zest, sugar, cumin, turmeric, cinnamon, fennel, salt, and mushroom or MSG powder (if using). Set aside.

In a cold skillet or sauté pan, combine the olive oil, garlic, and ginger. Place over medium heat and cook gently, stirring continuously, until golden and fragrant. Stir in the almonds and pepitas and continue cooking until the garlic is pale golden and the nuts are just starting to color.

Remove from the heat, then push everything to one side of the pan and carefully tip the fried shallots, chopped dates, and the spice mixture into the cleared side of the pan. You should hear a sizzle! Stir until the spices are fragrant, then combine everything thoroughly. Taste and season with salt. Let the mixture cool, then transfer it to a clean pint jar. The chili crisp is ready right away, but for optimal flavor, let it stand overnight. Store in the refrigerator and consume within 10 days.

DATE PALAPA

ABOUT 2 CUPS [480 G]

Caveat 1: This is based on a condiment from the Philippines and the dates are a very nontraditional inclusion. Caveat 2: As with the other condiment recipes in this chapter with unwieldy ingredient lists, this will still taste good even if you have trouble sourcing all the ingredients, but it is truly spectacular when made as written, I promise.

You can often find fresh makrut lime leaves at Asian grocery stores. If you can't find them, you can substitute the zest of a regular lime, but it will not be the same.

Grated or shredded fresh coconut can be found in the freezer section of many of the same places that will sell you makrut lime leaves. If you can find it, toast as described in the recipe—it makes for a chewier, more toothsome texture than dried flake coconut, but both are delicious.

Finally, if you don't have any white pepper you can use black, but I love the barnyard funk of white pepper against the rich coconut and sweet dates.

Date Palapa is good with eggs, fish, tacos, rice, and beans. Honestly, the only thing I've tried that wasn't improved by it was a michelada. Everything else is illuminated by this vat of gold.

1 cup [60 g] large flake, unsweetened dried coconut

¼ cup [60 ml] neutral oil

10 garlic cloves, very finely minced

One 3 in [7.5 cm] piece fresh ginger, peeled and finely minced

1 cup [100 g] finely chopped scallions, white and green parts

2 to 9 fresh red chiles (calibrate the heat level to your taste!), thinly sliced

6 makrut lime leaves, center ribs removed and leaves chiffonaded into confetti-like threads

3 large or 6 small dates, pitted and roughly chopped

1 Tbsp fish sauce

White pepper

In a small skillet over medium heat, toast the coconut, stirring continuously, until it is a deep golden brown. Take the coconut as far as you dare, to the very edge of burnt (but don't actually burn it). Transfer the coconut to a bowl.

Return the skillet to medium heat and add the oil. Add the garlic, ginger, and scallions and cook until fragrant, about 3 minutes. Stir in the chiles, lime leaves, dates, and fish sauce until combined, then add a generous grind of white pepper and the toasted coconut and cook, stirring occasionally, until everything is golden and deliciously fragrant, another 5 minutes. Let the mixture cool, then transfer it to a clean pint jar. Let it stand for at least 15 minutes and preferably overnight so the flavors can combine. The palapa will keep in a jar in the refrigerator, covered in oil, for up to a week.

UMM QAIS'S GRILLING SPICES

ABOUT 1 CUP [240 G]

A powerful blend! I use this rub to make Dry-Brined Roast Duck with Cumin & Fennel Seeds (page 120), but you can use it on any protein you like. I've had particular success with lamb chops covered in the rub and left to rest in the fridge for 12 hours before grilling—the smoke and char make for an unspeakably good al fresco dining experience, with very tender meat. This is because the date sugar acts as a tenderizer, drawing moisture out of the meat and seasoning it in tandem with the salt.

This spice blend is also great with firm tofu, mushrooms, grilled or roasted vegetables, and on eggs. My favorite unexpected use for it is as a popcorn sprinkle.

¾ cup [100 g] date sugar

¼ cup [35 g] flaky salt, such as Maldon

2 tsp fruity and mild red chili flakes, such as Urfa biber

1 tsp whole fennel seeds

1 tsp whole cumin seeds

In a medium bowl, stir together the date sugar, salt, chili flakes, fennel, and cumin until completely combined. Store in a clean jar in a cool and dry place. The grilling spices will keep for many months.

DIBS BARBECUE SAUCE

ABOUT 2 CUPS [480 G]

If you use this as a glaze, as with the Barbecue Mushroom Steaks with Cornbread Crumbles (page 110), thin it out by combining one part sauce to two parts water before brushing it on, to prevent burning while cooking. Serve at full strength if you're using it as a condiment. It's excellent with chicken nuggets, for the most discerning of toddlers.

One 14 oz [400 g] can fire-roasted tomatoes

½ cup [120 ml] date molasses

3 Tbsp apple cider vinegar

3 Tbsp Worcestershire sauce

1 Tbsp sweet smoked paprika

½ tsp salt

½ tsp freshly ground black pepper

½ tsp finely ground espresso powder (optional)

½ tsp ground cumin

½ tsp mustard powder

¼ tsp dried oregano

In a standard blender or using an immersion blender, whizz together the tomatoes, date molasses, vinegar, Worcestershire sauce, paprika, salt, pepper, espresso powder (if using), cumin, mustard powder, and oregano until smooth.

In a small saucepan over medium heat, bring the mixture to a simmer. Continue simmering, using a heatproof spatula to stir continuously and scrape down the sides of the pan, until the foam on top darkens from salmon-colored to a deep brick red, a finger run along the back of the spatula leaves a clear trail in the sauce, and big, lazy bubbles start to squelch and sputter, about 20 minutes. Let cool, then transfer to a clean jar. The barbecue sauce is ready right away, but it's even better cooled, refrigerated, and allowed to rest overnight for the flavors to develop. It will keep, in an airtight container in the refrigerator, for a couple of weeks.

DATE, FETA & LAVENDER RELISH

ABOUT 1½ CUPS [360 G]

Lavender can play a wonderful role in savory dishes, and in this relish it performs somewhat like rosemary. The first time I cooked a birthday meal for my now-husband, he asked me to make him roast duck with lavender potatoes, a combination he thought might be good. (He was right.) That being said, the lavender isn't going to make or break this condiment—you can experiment with swapping out any of the herbs, using fresh or dried, and it will still be delicious.

For a variation that stretches this relish into a side dish, chop 1 to 2 heads of broccoli into tiny florets. Peel the stalks and cut them into thin slices. Add all of the broccoli to the bowl with the spices and pepitas, then pour over the hot oil. Increase the lime juice to 2 table-spoons and let rest for at least an hour to give the broccoli time to cure.

2 fat garlic cloves, grated with a Microplane or very finely minced

2 tsp sweet smoked paprika

1 tsp fresh thyme leaves

1 tsp fresh oregano leaves

½ tsp fresh or dried lavender buds

Pinch of chili flakes (optional)

⅓ cup [40 g] pepitas or flaked almonds

⅓ cup [80 ml] olive oil

1 Tbsp fresh lime juice

8 dates, pitted and roughly chopped

7 oz [200 g] feta cheese

Salt

In a heatproof medium bowl, stir together the garlic, paprika, thyme, oregano, lavender, and chili flakes (if using).

In a small dry skillet over medium heat, toast the pepitas or almonds, stirring continuously, until fragrant and starting to turn golden brown, 3 to 4 minutes. Add the pepitas or almonds to the garlic and spice mixture.

In the same skillet, heat the olive oil over medium heat until just shimmering, being careful not to overheat it. Pour the oil over the garlic and spice mixture. The oil should crackle and sizzle, and the garlic and spices should immediately fill the air with appetizing aromas. Stir in the lime juice and the chopped dates. Crumble in the feta, in chunks roughly the same size as the dates— some larger bits, some smaller bits. Season with salt. The relish is ready right away, but it benefits from a rest—an hour at room temperature is good, but overnight in the refrigerator is better. Take the relish out of the refrigerator about 30 minutes before serving to remove the chill. The relish will keep, in an airtight container in the refrigerator, for up to 5 days.

HOT DATE! BUTTER

ONE 4 OZ [115 G] LOG COMPOUND BUTTER

A green and herbaceous, garlic-inflected, date-studded situation, friend to all carbs. Toss this with any format of potato (see Tater Tots Tossed in Hot Date! Butter, page 60) or smear on a baguette for an extra-amped garlic bread, perfect for spaghetti night. Skillet gnocchi! Hot rice! Over toast, under a crackly fried egg! Slice a bit off the log and set it to melt atop a perfectly seared steak!

Also: I know I am constantly pushing my Big Popcorn Agenda, but don't knock it until you try it. Gently melt a spoonful or two of this butter and toss through a big bowl of freshly popped popcorn for a stupendous snack.

5 Tbsp [75 g] butter, at room temperature

3 Tbsp olive oil

5 fat garlic cloves, grated with a Microplane or very finely minced

3 Medjool dates, pitted and finely chopped

½ cup [45 g] grated Parmesan cheese

1 large handful finely chopped soft fresh herbs (parsley, chives, scallion greens, ramps)

1 tsp lemon zest

¼ tsp salt

Freshly ground black pepper

In a medium bowl, mash together the butter, oil, garlic, dates, Parmesan, herbs, lemon zest, salt, and a good grind of pepper. Taste and adjust the seasoning. You can use this butter right away—the olive oil will keep it spreadable at room temperature—or store it for later by rolling it tightly into a parchment paper log (twist the ends like you're wrapping a piece of candy) and chilling it in the refrigerator for up to a week. If you'd like to keep it for longer, you can freeze the butter; just be sure to completely wrap the parchment log in plastic wrap so it doesn't get freezer burn.

WALNUTS IN DATE HONEY

ABOUT 2 CUPS [240 G]

A jar of sunshine, with endless uses. Serve this with labneh on toast, as part of a cheese plate, tucked inside a blanket of puff pastry, or as a topping for baked Brie. It's also lovely over yogurt at breakfast, as a curious side for roast meats, stuffed into cored apples and baked until the apples slump into their honeyed juices, or as a sort of relish for a summer fruit salad, tumbled with strawberries and basil.

1 Tbsp olive oil

6 oz [170 g] raw walnut halves

¼ cup [40 g] dates, pitted and roughly chopped

1 rosemary sprig

Zest of 1 lemon, peeled using a vegetable peeler into long thick strips (optional)

½ tsp flaky salt

1 cup [240 ml] mild honey, such as clover or acacia

In a large skillet or sauté pan over medium heat, warm the olive oil. Add the walnuts in a single layer and toast, stirring frequently, until golden and fragrant, 7 to 10 minutes. Be careful not to let the walnuts burn. Remove from the heat and roughly chop the walnuts. Transfer to a large bowl, then add the dates, rosemary,

lemon peel (if using), and salt and stir to combine. Pour in the honey and mix very thoroughly. Let cool, then transfer to a clean jar. The honey is ready right away but will keep, at room temperature, for up to 10 days.

BURNT DATE HONEY

ABOUT ½ CUP [120 ML]

Much like browning butter, taking your relationship with date molasses to the next level (burnt) adds complexity to its already-intriguing flavor profile. Burning date molasses gives it a rounded, compelling bitterness, like the darkest of chocolate or blackest of coffee.

A spoonful makes a superb mixer in a cocktail. You can also drizzle it over plain cheesecake, serve it with a cheese plate, use it to marinate summer stone fruit, make it the base of a salad dressing, stir it into your breakfast tahini instead of regular date molasses (see the Shami breakfast spread on pages 76 and 77), or use it to sweeten hot chocolate instead of sugar—be sure to drape some more over the cap of whipped cream. Best of all, burnt date honey can be drizzled over a slice of spicy pepperoni pizza. You're welcome.

½ cup [120 ml] date molasses
Big pinch of salt (optional)

Pour the date molasses into a small, high-sided saucepan and set over medium-high heat. Affix a candy thermometer to the side of the pan or have one handy nearby. Bring to a simmer, then turn the heat to low and cook, stirring frequently with a heat-proof (preferably silicone) spatula, for

5 minutes. Remove the molasses from the heat when it hits 340°F [170°C]. Look for lots of tiny bubbles; the molasses will start to pull away from the bottom of the pan, leaving a clear line traced by your spatula's path. The molasses should visibly darken in color from dibs brown to a deep, almost black, color. It will smell pleasantly burnt and caramelized.

Off the heat, stir in 2 tablespoons of water until completely blended—watch out, as the molasses may foam up. Stir in the salt (if using), then let cool. Transfer to a sterilized jar. The honey will keep indefinitely in a cool, dark place.

A BLACK TREE A PALM TREE BLACK and INKY LiKE A TOWER THE SiLK of TREES

from the ARAB APOCALYPSE by ETEL ADNAN

STUFFED DATES: SOME NOTIONS

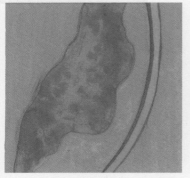

'NDUJA + CANDIED ORANGE PEEL

MANCHEGO CHEESE + QUINCE PASTE

SPICED LABNEH + CHESTNUT

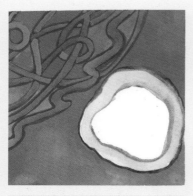

CARAMELIZED ONIONS + GOAT CHEESE

BIG CRUNCHY GARLICKY CROUTON

PLANTAIN CHIP + LIME + CREMA + CILANTRO

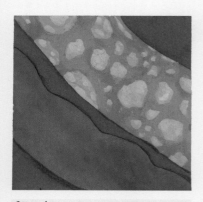

CHORIZO + ROASTED RED PEPPER

HALLOUMI + ZA'ATAR

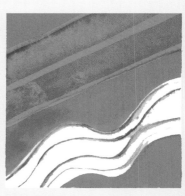

GUAVA PASTE + CREAM CHEESE

Sweet

ROSE PETAL + LEMON CREAM

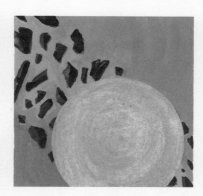

ALMOND BUTTER + CACAO NIBS

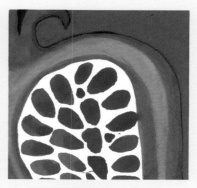

POMEGRANATE SEEDS

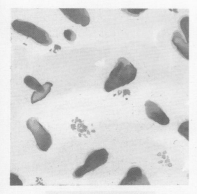

PISTACHIO HALWA

BANANA + WHIPPED CREAM + CHERRY

CANDIED CITRUS PEEL

PEANUT BUTTER + JAM + CHOCOLATE

MARZIPAN!

LYCHEE + STRAWBERRY + MINT

SUGGESTED MENUS

Spring

**DATE BLOSSOMS, SALTY, SEXY, RIPE
FOR PLUCKING. SUGAR AND SYRUP**

Fennel Ribbons with Salty Peanuts
Brown Butter Scallops
Peas with Mint & Preserved Lemon
Butter-Roasted Radishes

Summer

KHALAL, TANNIC, CRUNCHY, CRISPY, YELLOW

Yellow Barhi & Green Apple Kale Salad
Rib Eye Steak with a Salt & Date Sugar Crust
Midsummer Salad
Summer Plums in Date Syrup
Summer Gold Fruit Salad

Autumn

RUTAB, RIPE, SOFT, YIELDING

Rutab & Summer Tomatoes with Sizzling Brown Butter
Beef Shank Rutabiyya with Preserved Lemon Gremolata
Mushrooms en Papillote with Much Garlic
Pomegranate Parfaits
Silky Chocolate-Date Truffles

Winter

TAMAR, DRIED, DARK, CHEWY

Double-Ginger Carrot Soup
Spicy Charred Sweet Potato Planks
Milk-Braised Lamb Shanks with Mughal Spices
Sticky Toffee Pudding
Winter Elixir

BRUNCH for 6

Pumpkin Pancakes with Warm Ras el Hanout Syrup
Ghisava, or Cupid's Omelet
Dragon Fruit & Cardamom Smoothies

IFTAR for 12

Jallab
Crispy Sautéed Dates on a Saffron Cloud
13-Hour Lamb with Date & Feta Relish
Whole Roasted Cauliflower with Briny Olive
     Oil–Cured Chiles
Black Desert Cake
Hot Mix Chocolate Chip Cookies, sent home with guests
     as a suhoor treat

WEEKNIGHT IFTAR for 2

Double-Ginger Carrot Soup
Macarouna bil Laban
Mabroosheh

FESTIVE DINNER for 4

Sesame-Crusted Halloumi
Shaved Celery Salad with Spiced Date Chili Crisp
Dry-Brined Roast Duck with Cumin & Fennel Seeds
Whole Roasted Pineapple Draped in Spiced Caramel

ON the COAL

Grilled Dates in Grapefruit & Paprika Oil
Malai Chicken with Creamy Stuffed Dates *or*
Kuwaiti Red Snapper with Onion Rice
Chocolate Sorbet with Warm Salted Dates

TEATIME

Sticky Date Masala Chai
Duck & Date Jam Sandos
Date & Cream Scones with Whipped
     Lemon-Vanilla Butter
Lime & Ginger Crunch

WHERE
TO SHOP

DATES

Fresh Dates by Anderson
Yellow barhis in season, for pickup in or near Thermal, California.
www.freshdatesbyanderson.com

Bateel
Dubai-based fancy date retailer, with some regional special-ties and innovative or unusual date products: jams, mustards, vinegars, and roasted date seed coffee.
https://bateel.com

Sphinx Date Ranch
Seasonal source for rare Arizona-grown Black Sphinx dates.
https://sphinxdateranch.com

Persian Basket
For saffron, Iranian flavors, dried fruit and nuts, Mazafati dates.
www.persianbasket.com

Rancho Meladuco Date Farm
Yellow Barhi dates in season, great California Medjools.
https://ranchomeladuco.com

Coachella's Best Organic Dates
Yellow Barhi dates in season.
https://coachellasbestdates.com

Sam Cobb Farms
Home of the Black Gold date, a unique varietal.
www.samcobbfarms.com

Date Lady
Date syrup and date sugar.
https://ilovedatelady.com

SPICES

SOS Chefs
The most magical store in New York City. Every kind of spice you can imagine, one million types of pepper and salt, rare and hard-to-find cheffy ingredients.
https://sos-chefs.com

Diaspora Co.
Turmeric, cumin, cardamom, ginger. Fair trade and equitable spices, some of the most potent and delicious I've found.
www.diasporaco.com

Burlap & Barrel
High-quality, ethically sourced spices from around the world.
www.burlapandbarrel.com

Kalustyan's
Since 1944, the go-to source for New Yorkers on the hunt for specialty food items of any kind. Ships nationwide.
https://foodsofnations.com

Daphnis and Chloe
Wild Greek herbs. I particularly love their oregano, wild thyme buds, smoked chili flakes, and fennel seeds.
https://daphnisandchloe.com

OTHER

Canaan Palestine
Olive oil from landrace varietals, za'atar, freekeh, and more, grown in Palestine on artisan family farms.
www.canaanpalestine.com

Mirzam Chocolate Makers
Date-related chocolate confections (and more!) from Dubai's first bean-to-bar chocolatier.
https://mirzam.com

Hashems
Ma'amoul molds and traditional kitchenware.
www.hashems.com

Sadaf
Good source for a variety of Middle Eastern (particularly Shami) ingredients, founded by a Palestinian family.
www.sadaf.com

Sahadi's
A Brooklyn go-to, originally founded in Manhattan's Little Syria in 1895 by a Lebanese family. Incredible source for spices, dried fruit and nuts, specialty cheeses, snacks, and treats.
www.sahadis.com

Ziyad Brand
Stocked in grocery stores nationwide, with a good range of Middle Eastern ingredients.
www.ziyad.com

Ziba Foods
Heirloom and wild-grown dried fruit and nuts, sustainably and ethically sourced in Afghanistan.
www.zibafoods.com

The
FRONDS
of the PALMS
WAVE in
the WIND

LIKE
DANCING
GIRLS
PULLING
ONE ANOTHER'S
TRESSES.

AL MARRAR IBN MUNQIDH

FOR ME,
LET THEM BRING IN
the MAN of MY HEART. LET THEM
BRING in to ME MY AMA-USHUMGAL-ANNA,
the POWER of the DATE PALM. LET THEM PUT HIS
HAND in my HAND, LET THEM PUT HIS HEART BY
MY HEART. AS HAND is PUT to HEAD, the
SLEEP is so PLEASANT. AS HEART is
PRESSED to HEART, the PLEASURE
is so SWEET. — from a
Kungar (sumerian religious song) to
INANNA, ancient Mesopotamian
goddess of love, beauty,
war & fertility.

ACKNOWLEDGMENTS

Andrianna deLone: This book would not exist without you. Thank you, thank you.

To the Chronicle team: Sarah Billingsley, you immediately saw the potential in this hot-pink-hot-date-kaleidoscopic-disco-oasis-cookbook-dreamhouse and made this book both real and true; Vanessa Dina, you not only saw the vision, but you also made the book both functional and beautiful. To the rest of the Chronicle team, thank you for all of your incredible work: Alex Galou, Jessica Ling, Tera Killip, Steve Kim, Lauren Salkeld, Elora Sullivan, Erica Gelbard, and Cappy Yarbrough.

Linda Xiao, Maeve Sheridan, Monica Pierini, and Megan Litt: I still don't understand the wild alchemy that allowed you to extract the perfect vision for each dish from within my brain and translate it into such magical photographs. Thank you for your willingness to get a little wacky with the shots, and for your talent and your joyfulness. Spending time on set with you was truly a gift.

I am lucky to be surrounded by good folks who are always ready to hype me (and my harebrained schemes) up. A thousand thank-yous to: Bettina Huang, CF forever and ever. Cutter and Erin and Teddy and Lula, my favorite Shwoods. Samia Husari, you are my rock. Evan James, for gassing me up: You are complicit in this situation. Adrienne Raphel, for Friday Breakfast Energy. Amy DeCicco and Jay Carlson. The Immortal Diamonds of Writing Groupe: Sara Akant, Ashley Colley, Katie Fowley, Callie Garnett, James of Longley, Dan Poppick, Bridget Talone. Paul Tourle, for your thoughtfulness and generosity and vivid imagination. Malek Bsat, for your early championship of this project and your enthusiasm, curiosity, and voracious appetite for food and design. The Snug in its vast and loving entirety: truly, the best pocket coven a gal could ask for. In particular: Felicity, Emma, Kase, Katina, and Kayleigh, for weighing in on the proposal. Sarah Lohman, for bringing the very first of the date recipes out into the world. Kannan Mahadevan and Marquis Facey, for being

willing test subjects and for giving the lacquered pineapple the reception it deserved. The Dubai contingent: Lateefa Bint Maktoum, Sahar Parham Al Awadhi, and Kathy Johnston, for hot (date) tips, recipes, and advice. Thank you to the California date growers who generously shared their time and expertise with me: Joan Smith, Janice and Allen Anderson, Sam and Maxine Cobb. CF Watkins, I don't know how it is that you always see me so clearly with your camera (and your heart), but thank you for bringing your many talents to bear in the taking of the dreaded author photo. Nick Appelbaum, Aki Carpenter, and everyone at RAA, thank you for helping me understand that a cookbook can be its own kind of museum.

Particular thanks to Tayyeb Zarouni and his date farmers, who showed us such hospitality, and who gave Qais his blossoms.

It takes a village to test a cookbook. Many, many thanks to everyone who gave their time and their tastebuds to test the recipes in the book: Ruchi Asher, Elizabeth Bertch, Bryan Chang, Cindy Chang & Adam Szym, Joni Dames, Anna Doukakis, Leslie Feinberg, Steve Hohne, Rhea Kumar, James Longley, Jeremy & Kathryn Medow, Mary-Brett O'Bryan, Marco Oliveri, Adrienne Raphel, Lily Remmert, Katina Rogers, Felicity Rose, Tamara Rushovich, Sarah Seekatz, Amanda Tamas, Laura Vitale, Allie White, Kase Wickman, and Emily Yoder. Vincent Traverso: Your attempted brewing of the Scoundrels' Wine was much appreciated despite the microbial bloom. Turns out tenth-century recipes might not be as easily adapted to today's kitchens as we thought.

My thanks and love to everyone in the family: Hashem & Isphana. Firas, Alexandra & Leo. Rasha, Tom & Lincoln. Faisal and Amy. Barbara, Doug, Hannah, Robby, and sweet Sybil. Villa and Lory and Rafeeq. Big Nani!

Finally, most importantly: Colby and Qais, loves of my life. This book is for you.

INDEX

E

F

Chronicle Books publishes distinctive books and gifts. From award-winning children's titles, bestselling cookbooks, and eclectic pop culture to acclaimed works of art and design, stationery, and journals, we craft publishing that's instantly recognizable for its spirit and creativity. Enjoy our publishing and become part of our community at www.chroniclebooks.com.